BIG BOOK OF MARRIAGE

UNPACKING GOD'S DESIGN FOR LIFELONG
COVENANT

DR. SCOTT SILVERII

LEAH SILVERII

Five
Stones
Press

CONTENTS

INTRODUCTION

Dear Readers,

Leah and I have prayed over writing this book for years. Through that time, we have been blessed to minister and counsel many married couples. This book reflects our own experiences and other couples we have helped along the way. We know this Big Book of Marriage will serve as a practical guide in strengthening your relationship.

We wrote this book shoulder-to-shoulder to make sure it speaks to both of you. Together, Leah and I agreed to share it with you from my first-person perspective just to make sure it is easier to read. So, when you read, "I said this or that," know it's from the both of us.

With all the challenges in marriage, we wanted to keep this book simple and to the point. Your marriage matters, so we wasted no time in getting you the answers to some of the toughest issues in relationships. We are praying for you and your marriage. God did not design it to fail. Do this His way and you have a 100% chance of success.

Marriage Matters,
Scott & Leah

PART I

1

PAIN AND HEALING

Pain may seem like an odd place to start a marriage book, but depending on what season your marriage is in, pain may be the perfect spot to dive in. The truth is, we all have had, have, or will experience pain in our relationships. No matter who you are, dealing with wicked stuff that just won't leave you alone is an unfortunate fact of life and love.

When we first started to mentor married couples, Leah and I would share affirming biblical foundations for making marriage great. We soon realized—because of the presence of past trauma and current pain in either one or both spouses—that the positive marriage talk was falling on deaf ears. We quickly shifted our focus toward helping spouses *heal* before we could help them *grow*.

This is why we feel tackling pain and healing is the best starting point for a marriage book.

Here's a little secret—***time does not heal all pain***. The wounds you carry into marriage will only fester, and the hurts suffered by marriage may compound the ones unattended to. Let's focus on pain first so we can get to the good stuff.

One pattern we've noticed in almost everyone we've mentored and counseled is that a major source of pain comes from childhood. Whether abandoned, abused, or neglected, most can trace the clues to what they are struggling with in their marriage to a period in their past that left such an indelible wound that it still radiates destruction today.

Marriage suffers when we fail to root out our source of pain and allow it to manifest itself as dissatisfaction with our spouse. Until there is healing, there will be no peace in your relationship. And until there is peace in your relationship, you will both suffer.

Pain comes in many forms, so let's take time to make sure we are healthy and healed enough to develop a solid foundation for marriage. And, if we can make a special plea to the guys (myself included), men tend to strap a false bravado around their necks and claim they're not hurting. Men associate being hurt with being weak, and that's not correct. Healing doesn't mean you are weak. It means you are smart. Be smart about staying strong!

Personal Profiles in Past Pain

What's really eating away at you? Do regrets consume your thoughts? Can't sit in silence without a mental movie flooding your mind and demanding you fill the quiet space with unhealthy thoughts? Do you stay busy just so memories or regrets can't catch or overcome you?

You're not alone. The pain we carry from our past is tucked

away and always available to muck up our lives or turn gold star moments into brown star disappointments. We allow pain, shame, and regret to overwhelm us with stress over how to cope with it. Unfortunately, the coping solves nothing. Healing does. Let's look at three common ways we try and often fail to deal with unresolved hurt.

Medication

God chose David to be king over Israel, but he didn't come to the throne without serious personal baggage. David's pain was rooted in the rejection by his father, Jesse. He wasn't considered worthy of meeting the prophet Samuel who was sent by God to anoint a ruler. Yet, there in that rejected, messed-up boy, Israel had a king. David's rejection by his father stung and stuck. Have you been hurt by a parent, and never forgiven them? This injury doesn't heal in time; it heals through forgiveness.

When we have no affirmation as kids, we tend to grow up seeking that love from someone—anyone. In David's case, he found that assurance in the women he slept with, but sex with one of his six wives wasn't enough. In the absence of affirmation, there is *never* a point of "enough."

David did his best to keep it between the lines, but his unresolved pain eventually became too much to bear. There are many ways to medicate our pain. Some use alcohol, drugs, sex, exercise, work, or any of many addictions to compensate for the hurt we feel from an emptiness caused by unresolved injury. King David relied on the most common form of "medication" for easing his past of rejection—sex.

Yes, even before there was a World Wide Web, sexual addiction was a major issue. David's sexual addiction led to his most public failure when his affair with Bathsheba led to the death of her spouse, loss of their child, and a legacy of family dysfunction. Medicating your pain with anything other than actual healing by getting to the root cause is only going to make the problem more complex, and eventually cost you your marriage.

Please understand that addiction is not the source of your problem. Your problem is that you're using your addiction (sex, drugs, alcohol, shopping etc.) to avoid healing from the source of your pain. God wants to heal you because He loves you. Allow yourself to heal. It's better than the hurt.

Motivation

The next false solution for dealing with pain is motivation. We'll look at the wisest and wealthiest man to have ever lived. Solomon was the son of David. Despite growing up in a household besieged with the consequences of David's sexual affair with his mother, Bathsheba, Solomon was loved by God and blessed tremendously. By today's standards, we'd think the guy had it made.

Unfortunately, Solomon's wounds drove him to prove himself daily. Performance-based relationships are tough on us as kids and still difficult as adults. If you felt you were only acknowledged and shown love as a child when you made good grades, or behaved, or if you felt that you had to earn your parents' or spouse's love, then you can relate to Solomon's performance-based relationship with his parents.

Motivation and achievements were Solomon's failed attempt to soothe his pain. The more accolades he accumulated to fill the void of love and security, the less deserving he felt. Our souls need peace, not prizes.

Leah and I can both attest to this failed form of hiding past pain. I rose through the ranks of law enforcement to become a chief of police, while also earning a master's degree and PhD. *Guess what?* With each height of accomplishment, the depth of my hurt only grew deeper and darker. Leah, who is a best-selling author with over ninety novels to her name, only grew more inward as her writing career skyrocketed. *Why?* Neither one of us addressed the cracked foundations that were the root of our pain, so we tried to out-achieve our healing with worldly accomplishments.

Meditation

There is a third unhealthy way of dealing with our hurt. Absalom was also David's son and Solomon's half brother. His pain, like many with a dominant parent, began at home. Once again, because of the family dysfunction linked to their dad's sexual sin, Absalom suffered from intense guilt over doing nothing to defend his sister from a sexual attack by another half brother.

How often do we find ourselves in a situation we know is wrong, yet we stand by silently as injustice unfolds? Even if we aren't the target of abuse, witnessing or being confided in can cause secondary trauma that, if not resolved, will continue to fester.

Meditation stewed in Absalom's soul until it boiled over into hatred. For two years he avoided healing from his wounds and forgiving the offender before it erupted in rage, and he killed his half brother. Absalom's deep-seated pain also led to rebellion against his father and, tragically, his own death.

Attacks against others is what defines Absalom. Are you feeling the wrath of regret and wrongdoings boil beneath the surface while you look for an outlet to unleash your fury? Do you booze it until you lose it, yet it's worse than when it began? Shutting down and climbing into silent corners as you stew over the latest attack is not going to resolve anything. It only reinforces the dysfunction of past relationships and places current strains on your marriage. No matter how hard it is, learn to say, "I'm sorry," quickly and stay engaged until the conflict is unwoven.

Pain Prevention

Marriage is a choice we make that's coupled with the choice to love the one we're married to, but pain is a different story. Seldom, no, actually never, do we choose to be hurt as a child. Being wounded is not something we sought out, but the choice to continue suffering from the pain is within our control.

Marriage is two imperfect people coming together to create a loving relationship, while working to help each other heal from past connections. Because personal pain isn't as obvious as the physical, it can lie dormant, but destructive, for years and prove toxic to your relationship.

Whether you carry the stripes of being abandoned by a parent through divorce, the domination of one parent over the entire family, or you've suffered physical, verbal, or sexual abuse, society's expectation forces us to suppress healing while heaping new pain atop the open wounds of our past. This toxic combination weighs heavy on our marriages.

Let's identify these areas and move toward recovery to make sure your marriage doesn't become a victim to past or current offenses. Unlike physical harm, emotional, mental, and spiritual injuries don't naturally heal over time. While the body launches into an immediate recovery phase after experiencing a physical wound, your spirit remains vulnerable. As a matter of fact, spiritual injuries grow more severe the longer left unattended.

It's worth repeating: ***Time does not heal all wounds.***

Without the tools to process trauma, we enter the danger zone for risky, irrational behaviors. Unchecked, this can easily send your life and marriage tragically off the rails. Many people refuse to be healed. You're probably thinking you read that wrong, but it's true. Not everyone is willing to do the work. Some get trapped in their affliction and allow it to become their identity.

There are several reasons people don't seek help. Intimidation and being ridiculed by others are the top two. You'd also be surprised to know that in this world of everything online, many people don't know where to start to get the help to heal.

So where should you begin? We always suggest first communicating openly and often with your spouse. A spouse usually already knows, but is too afraid to ask because you've not provided a safe landing for vulnerable discussions. They've become conditioned by how you shut them out, dismiss them, or deflect the conversation. And if they push too hard, you become angry. So, they learn to walk on eggshells. Don't be the strong, silent, and suicidal type—get help.

Disassociation Tactics

Disassociation is a tactic we use to distance ourselves from the act that hurt us. But even if the distance is physical space and time, the tether that ties you to that source of pain is always attached. Besides, you can't selectively shut off one emotion without adversely affecting other emotions. It's usually a spouse who suffers when we try to manipulate emotional integrity. Let's talk about three important emotions you must be aware of that are necessary and part of dealing with pain.

Anger

When you delay healing from pain through denial, you'll discover anger has been waiting to rage for a while. This anger also has two options—to manifest internally or externally. Anger and revenge are usually directed at whoever it was that hurt you. Restoration is a much better option. In the absence of the original source of anger, we then zero in on whoever is closest and most vulnerable to our outrage—our spouse.

Oftentimes, we turn that anger inward because we don't want to confront the offender or show we're vulnerable through being hurt. We begin to internalize shame, guilt, or depression for allowing ourselves to have been victimized.

Before you destroy yourself or your marriage, consider asking for help to process your anger. Smashing chairs in the house doesn't resolve your pain, it only leaves you with nowhere to sit. Seek help. Remember this from Ephesians 4:26: Anger is not a sin, if you don't sin in your anger.

Grieving

Grieving is important for allowing a balance to anger. It usually begins as the process of anger is resolved or managed. We usually don't bother taking the time to understand that grieving is a natural and necessary part of maintaining a healthy life. We're usually in a *go get 'em* mode with no time to grieve. But grief is going to find you somewhere along the line, like it or not. Why not take the opportunity to manage it before things go too far?

Grieving isn't only a by-product of someone else's death. It might hit during a career change, childbirth or empty nesting, or a shift in a significant relationship. You might be grieving the potential loss of your marriage, child visitation, or your job. All these events are accompanied by emotion, and emotions require processing.

You may feel as though these days are your darkest and you can't hold on any longer. Allow us to assure you that you can make it to the light at the end of the tunnel. What's also great is that God gives us an incredible partner to make that journey toward freedom. Your spouse is the best partner you'll ever have. Learn to lean on them when times are tough.

Getting back to being healthy and happy is waiting for you, but the denial, anger, disassociation, and every layer of separation between the reality of what harmed you has created a barrier. Now is the time to tear down that wall between you and the healing grace of Jesus Christ so that grieving personal pain may begin.

Acceptance

Rarely are we harmed by strangers. When the hurt comes from someone we know, the pain is so much more intense due to the loss of innocence and the betrayal of the trust we had in that person. There is an expected honor code of adult protector that's violated when the protector becomes the predator.

That violation not only leaves soul scars because of what actions were perpetrated, but trust was broken as well. The physical body can heal itself or be healed. Soul scars are very different, and responses to violations of trust hurt deeper than broken bones or bruises.

Moving beyond grief and into healing, we do begin to experience an acceptance of the ugly realities of life. No, we're not happy with it, but we do land on a level ground of peace or contentment.

Breaking Free from Past Pain

Can you remain married yet still harbor deep pockets of past personal pain? Yes, you can, but why would you remain in bondage if there are avenues for regaining freedom? So many of us suffer with poor health, anxiety, addictions, and depression. Our spouses also suffer from the effects of secondary exposure to our hurting. Buried beneath pits of pain isn't the fertile soil for a happy marriage.

There are a few areas we'd like to discuss as you both prepare to tackle the strongholds standing just on the other side of freedom from past pain. The first is an important concept to understand—surrender. We know that most people think of surrender as waving the white flag. This isn't a case of quitting, but it is an opportunity to take a step away from a losing battle to regain focus. Think of it as a reset, not a retreat.

Surrender

While putting up a valiant effort and resisting the enemy is encouraged, surrendering our lives to Jesus Christ is an act of love and trust. Sacrificial love is the highest expression there is. God gave up His one and only beloved Son so that we may know everlasting life through salvation. We are asked to surrender our sinful, selfish desires to God so that He may guide us to a deep relationship with Him, our spouse, and others.

Why doesn't God just make us listen and obey Him, you might ask? That's a great question. God loves us so dearly that He gave us free will. How could we freely love someone if we were forced to do so? Free will is what separates us from the animals. Unfortunately, free will is also what's caused us all our troubles, beginning with Adam and Eve. We have the freedom to surrender to the one who will set us free from our troubled lives, or we can continue to cling to relationship after broken relationship.

Soul Ties

Soul ties are God's invisible miracle of creating long-lasting bonds of relationship that go deeper than surface-level experiences. Have you ever met someone for the first time, and it was like a light came on in your soul? We're not talking about a romantic connection, but yeah, that happens too.

We think about the reaction when Mary went to visit Elizabeth in the New Testament. They were respectively pregnant with Jesus and John (the Baptist). Elizabeth's baby jumped in her womb at the sound of Mary's voice. There was a tie between Jesus and John the Baptist who would meet again and change the history of the world.

Another thought that we always associate with a positive soul tie is the brotherhood of David and Jonathan. David had seven biological brothers, and Jonathan was the son of King Saul, who set out to kill David as he would become king of

Israel. Despite both factors, these men were closer than brothers.

As soon as he had finished speaking to Saul, the soul of Jonathan was knit to the soul of David, and Jonathan loved him as his own soul.

1 Samuel 18:1

While soul ties can be positive bonds to old friends and family, they are also spiritual attachments to events, actions, images, or anything that has trapped you in that moment in time that just won't allow you to be free to move forward with your life. Sort of like Monday afternoons at work!

Soul ties can also start off bad and get worse. Maybe you were sexually assaulted as a child by a friend or relative. That sin-based connection can control the rest of your life because of the tether to a wrong relationship. Some other soul ties are bonded through addiction, guilt, and obligation, to name a few. Anything that has attached itself and still influences your thoughts, emotions, or actions is a soul tie.

Satan is skilled at perverting our memories of past relationships. Have you noticed that when you and your spouse fight, your mind starts to go back to past relationships? Maybe that ex-spouse wasn't so bad. Maybe it was me, or I wonder if she's still available? The reason these thoughts take hold is because you've never severed the negative soul tie from your spirit. The good news is that you have the authority to pray over every one of the bonds that keep you chained to the past, and slice right through them.

It's important that if you haven't already identified what it is that haunts you, to really begin praying over this. Ask God to reveal to you what it is in your spirit that you need to be freed from. You have the supernatural authority to cut negative soul ties.

Some of us visualize these spiritual ties as strands, like spiderwebs stretching from that moment in the past to where we are today. When I began to understand the concept of soul ties, I immediately saw my past pain connected to my spirit by giant suspension-bridge cables. The violent trauma of almost three decades in law enforcement only compounded the childhood abuse I survived. I had no choice but to free myself from these corrupted soul ties if there was any hope of being free and healed.

It might sound funny if this is your first exposure to the reality of soul ties, but once you begin to pray over them, you will start to "see" yourself still supernaturally connected to your past. Like I said, my soul ties were so powerfully destructive over the course of my life that they were like thick, impenetrable cables. But, as I prayed God's authority over them, they were sliced like a hot knife through butter. The point is, we can muddle through life without ever scratching that itch, or we can rid ourselves of the darkness, and move forward with living the blessed life that God created for us.

Inner Vows

Inner vows are common among most people. We make them as kids, teens, and young adults. They range from what we'll be when we grow up, to who we'll marry, to what type of job we'll secure. They also turn into negative attachments when we vow to never love again.

I'll never be poor.

I'll never spank my kids like I was spanked.

I'll never *fill in the blank.*

These are inner vows, and you might not even realize you've made them. While these can be meant as aspirations and life goals, the critical point is that they can become destructive because of the emotional framework being erected outside of God's will for our life.

Let's take a quick step back and define just what an inner vow is so we're on the same page. Inner vows are a self-oriented commitment made in response to a person, experience, or desire in life.

When we are hurt, especially earlier in life, it's not uncommon to respond emotionally in anger with an inner vow to curse something or avoid the source of that pain. If we were whipped by a parent, and it embarrassed us, then it would be an expected response as a child to vow to never whip or discipline our own kids. While that might sound like a noble gesture at the time, the reality is that a parent who refuses to discipline will produce unruly kids without structure. Not to mention your spouse, who may grow frustrated by your refusal to take charge of the kids.

The truth is, you probably don't remember making that inner vow as a young child while on the receiving end of a leather belt. But the reality is, once you make these self-directed statements, you have the potential for igniting a pattern of dysfunction and misery.

Other common inner vows are:

I'll never let anyone hurt me again.

I'll never be poor like my parents.

I'll never trust anyone again.
I'll never discipline my kids.
I'll never let my spouse talk to me that way.

Do any of those sound familiar? You should take the time to write out your own, but for now, think through the times you may have purposefully or inadvertently made inner vows out of embarrassment, anger, or frustration. The danger is with the self-oriented intention.

Because we are focusing on freeing ourselves from past personal pain, inner vows not only imprint a pattern of self-reliance, but from the moment of that vow, we're tethered to that past event. The irony is that whatever you promised to escape, flee from, or avoid earlier in life, will usually continue to haunt you because you're chained to it via the inner vow. Like soul ties, they can and must be broken to move forward and be free from the effects of pain.

Pain hurts, and it can also hurt to heal from pain. So many of us think that if we can just be happy for a while, the pain will go away. Short-term thinking will never solve chronic pain. If you married with the hopes of your spouse being the answer to what ails you, chances are, you've now exponentially compounded your problems.

The good news is that we're often attracted to those we feel can help us in the healing process. It's part of the attraction process God has designed so that we complement each other in our strengths and weaknesses. The best news though, is that

God is always at the ready to hear your cries for help and healing.

If you try to suck it up and play through the pain, what you'll eventually experience is that it starts to seep out at the most inopportune times. You'll become hypersensitive in low-priority discussions with your spouse that lead to blowout arguments. Spikes in anger and lingering resentment will cause seeds of doubt to be planted in your mind about whether or not you married the right person, and well, you get the picture.

Unresolved pain occurs when we hold on to the hurt by refusing to forgive our spouse. It's not always the big things that create this deep agony between loved ones. But over time, things like misunderstandings, misspending of finances, cutting comments, or silent treatments start to build up.

Forgiveness is the immediate cure. When you screw up, apologize and ask for forgiveness. When your spouse catches the short straw, make sure to forgive as you have been forgiven.

Today's high-risk society presents a serious challenge for hardening your exterior to trauma from outside forces. It also begins a desensitization process where your emotions become shielded as a form of self-preservation. It won't take long until this hard shell becomes a constant way of life. While you may notice the changes in the way of being better able to handle the stress of life, your spouse only sees someone they no longer recognize.

Pain mustn't be allowed to drive a wedge between the two of you. It can become a barrier, not only in communication, but in the desperately needed intimacy you both need to remain a strong, united team.

Sometimes we see the pain we suffer as a noble badge of honor. Like it's some righteous price we pay to protect our loved ones. We have a choice to either continue the path of unresolved pain and expect for it to deconstruct anything positive in our lives with an almost certain guarantee of dysfunction, or we can drop the rogue routine and get the help we need to live a fantastic life as a loving spouse. Trust us, your spouse will thank you.

Healing

Like most things in life, there is a process involved with healing. Just in case you are curious why God doesn't snap His fingers and make your pain go away, it's important to understand the different types of healing.

Instant Healing by Miracle:

There are countless examples of immediate healings performed by Jesus or through His disciples. They were quick and seemed effortless. Despite the various ailments, the common factor, besides God, was that those healed believed in the power to be healed. They were miracles and occurred not because of how good or bad the person was, but because that was the process by which God chose to heal them.

Healing by Process:

Whether healing is instant or occurs over a long period of time, it is the process for restoration. God sets the pace of restoration. What is important is that God's Word promises the result, not how long it takes.

How often have we passed through a trial, and once it's over, we've either forgotten what we'd been through, or come to understand changes in our lives because of having gone through something? Part of God's healing process is education.

Remember when Lazarus's family begged Jesus to run to him? What did Jesus do? He took four days before He arrived at the tomb of His friend. Lazarus had even begun to rot, and his flesh stunk, but Jesus was in no hurry. Why wasn't He?

There was a process. There were people besides Lazarus who would benefit in faith through this process, and while the result was imminent, the process vetted out doubts, fears, and hope from those attached to the process. Read John 11:1–46 for yourself and mark down how many people close to Christ behaved less than faithfully.

Just as in the example of Lazarus being raised from the dead, there are feelings present during the process of healing. No matter how hard we try to pretend we don't have feelings, the truth is we do. It doesn't mean we have to weep at the coffee shop or gym, but the process of healing from past personal pain involves our being able to understand why we feel the way we do.

Our spouse senses this hurt and the need to heal. They do not see this as weakness. Let me repeat this part—they do not see our need to heal as us being weak. That need is our human-ity, and our loved ones desperately need to see that character trait illustrated in their beloved. If we're willing to open up, you'll understand that they become the one best suited to help us heal from what ails us. God created us to become one team for making each a best version of ourselves. Be that team!

2

THE FIVE STONES OF MARRIAGE

It wasn't until Leah and I found marriage mentors who took the time to teach us about the importance of having each other's best interests, that our relationship began to become indestructible.

We call it the "Five Stones of Your Rock-Solid Marriage," and it's made the difference between just being married and having an amazing partnership as husband and wife. We want to share these five foundational stones with you because not only are they simple to honor, but they will add marital strength to your relationship like nothing else can.

Let's start with the reality that there is no such thing as the perfect marriage. You get out of it what you're both willing to put into it. Statistically, fewer people marry each year, yet the divorce rate remains consistently too high. We marry with the hope of spending our lives together. No one says, "I do," to experience a mediocre marriage or the devastation of divorce. This is the beginning of that hope for amazing!

Stone 1—STAND

This is where it all begins. **Standing** is so vital that it's one of the first items addressed in the garden of Eden with the original marriage between Adam and Eve. You each swore an oath to stand together in holy matrimony, now will you both continue to make a **stand** together in life?

That is why a man leaves his father and mother and is united to his wife, and they become one flesh.

Genesis 2:24

The relationship you share with each other was created by design to have no equal, outside of God of course. Not even your kids, your mom, or the friends on social media should compare to the priority you place on each other. You were designed to be each other's safe harbor and fiercest defender. Allow your spouse to be your priority and everything else in life will fall into balance.

When times get tough, we tend to tell others that they just don't understand what it's like. Ever heard that one? I've never been to the moon, but it doesn't mean I wouldn't love listening to an astronaut talk about space exploration. It's the same thing with married couples. There's no reason to withhold information from each other. This doesn't mean a massive data dump when you walk through the door, but it also doesn't mean you should prevent them from the opportunity to share the events (good and bad) in your life.

We can guarantee, you're telling somebody about what's happening in your life. It might not be your spouse, but you are talking to someone. It's natural, and how we process. The reality is, whoever that person is, even if it's your high school bud or your parents, they are not your spouse. Your spouse stands by you and should be prioritized in your daily life.

This is why God addressed men in verse 24: "...*a man leaves his father and mother...*" God knows a man's nature, and a big part of that nature is holding on to tethers that separate him from what really is important—his spouse. It's not just in marriage, men do it with everything.

Can you be completely naked before your spouse?

Yeah, we thought that might get your attention. What we're talking about is being naked in complete openness, transparency, and accountability. It's impossible to say that your stance supports marriage when one or both of you have secrets. This is where so many marriages fall apart. We try to pocket our secret sins for later just in case. Secrets are intimacy killers, and no intimacy soon leads to no marriage.

Those secrets develop because there is a space between spouses created when our foundational stance is out of whack. It's also where jealousy erupts into suspicion. Jealousy is not a bad thing. But we're not talking about keys-scratched-into-your-car-door type of jealousy. The righteous jealousy as God displays is healthy in a marriage. It's a protective posture once your spouse is the focus in your life.

Jealousy is protecting what is yours. And to be very clear, you each belong to the other, and deserve to be fought over, not fought against. You do not belong to your friends, co-workers, or that old flame back in high school. You are two to become one. If you're not at the "oneness" stage yet, then this is the perfect place to be. It took us a while to understand it, and once there, it has changed our lives and marriage.

We naturally begin to drift toward what interests us. Some lean toward career and achievement, while others focus on the home and family. There's nothing wrong with these pursuits unless they knock your stance off balance.

It's important to remain aware that your spouse is the most important person in your life. Everything else will fall into place when you show them that you are committed to remaining grounded in a stance based on God's Word for honoring them and the marriage.

How to STAND:

Remain on solid, level ground so that all decisions are based on truth and not temptation or emotion.

Keep both feet on the ground by understanding that your stance affects your spouse. Remaining grounded allows each to know they are safe and secure in the relationship.

Allow both "knees" to remain bent and flexible so that you both can respond and adjust to the changing seasons and challenges that life brings into marriage. Bent knees together in prayer are a great way to improve your stance.

Stone 2—TENSION

When in doubt, hold on tight. That's the advice we were given and the advice we give when it comes to tough times in life and marriage. The problem isn't with the holding on, but with the intensity with which it is held. We tend to strangle an issue out of fear, the unknown, or anger. Understanding the proper degree of tension with which to hold on allows for a proper grip in handling the situation. It also prevents dominating the issue instead of resolving it.

Marriage requires an active hands-on approach rather than trying to dominate or control everything. Most couples make the mistake of thinking that after the big wedding blowout, they simply do marriage. When problems arise, and they will, couples try to control them by suffocating them with their own ideas based on past perspectives, or they go hands off altogether. Neither works for marriage.

Once we've committed to the proper, solid stance of having our spouse's best interest at heart, we must apply the proper tension for addressing each situation as a team. The best way to know how to handle challenges is by talking to each other about the problem. We're too quick to jump in and try to fix it every time our spouse expresses frustration.

Sometimes, one spouse doesn't want or need the other one to fix it. They simply want you to listen. Other times, you're the problem and require adjusting your own degree of tension without fear of letting go or dropping the ball. No matter what the hurdles are in your relationship, a willingness to properly apply an active hold of the solution shows that you are each engaged in working together toward peace and a solid marriage.

A final word about tension. We are told often that one of the reasons spouses fight is they claim to have fallen out of love. You can no more fall out of love than you can become a cat. Love is not a feeling to ebb and flow. Love is a choice. Saying you fell out of love and now want a divorce is like selling your car because you ran out of gas. No, you don't give it up, you take hold, dig in, and adjust the tension. Then refill that love tank!

Stone 3—OBSERVATION

We're going to focus on this as it relates to seeing marriage for what it really is. If your marriage is messed up, then set your sights on making it right. If you're blessed with a powerful relationship, then amen for both of you, but let's continue to focus on keeping it tight and protected.

A big part of observing is having the single vision of relationship. You focus is on one target, and that is your marriage. If you start looking elsewhere, this is when your center is off and bad things happen. Part of that single vision focus on marriage is understanding that you and your spouse now share everything in life.

The old joke about what's yours is mine and what's mine is mine unfortunately still holds true in many marriages. When we enter a marriage covenant with God, sole possession of everything, and we mean everything, goes out the window. Your money, your debt, your favorite chair, your hobbies, your addictions, your magazines, your kids (yes, we said kids), your sins, and even your own body no longer belong solely to you. Remember when we talked about the two becoming one (Genesis 2:24)? Well, this is where it happens.

The husband should fulfill his marital duty to his wife, and likewise the wife to her husband. The wife does not have authority over her own body but yields it to her husband. In the same way, the husband does not have authority over his own body but yields it to his wife.

1 Corinthians 7:3–4

Gaining a godly observation of your marriage helps you to see that God has established a marital structure with Christ as the head, then the husband, and then the wife following her husband's spiritual headship. This Scripture is where we often get the disgruntled scoffs from the wives because it may appear at first look that the husband is the boss. Nothing could be further from spiritual reality. Servant leadership and sacrificial love distinguish the marital hierarchy from the world's understanding of being the boss.

But I want you to understand that the head of every man is Christ, the head of a wife is her husband, and the head of Christ is God.

1 Corinthians 11:3

The key to clear observation is to show that through submitting one to another, we surrender ourselves so we each hold equal possession of everything. Two-as-one also isn't saying we have $100 in the bank, so we each get $50. That's splitting community property. A true vision sees that you both have ownership of the same $100.

It's not uncommon to bring self-preservation tendencies to the table after you've been burned in a prior relationship. Escaping divorce with the clothes on your back forces people to develop a protective perspective of not losing what little survived while fleeing the fire of a failed marriage. It can make us hesitant to lay out all our chips.

But repeating past mistakes isn't the way to see this relationship grow. Having a single focus is the key to freely giving of yourselves to each other. Whether it's time, talent, or cash; there's always a reciprocating benefit to giving of yourself. Now it's time to give up any selfish visions each may have that no longer contribute to protecting your marriage's best interest. Learning to observe your relationship as it truly is fosters opportunities for improvements toward a beautifully strong relationship.

Stone 4—NAVIGATION

One of the biggest issues with married couples is they don't know how spouses are supposed to behave. Maybe you're modeling what you saw your parents do or you're trying to imitate what you've seen in the movies or television. If you've been married before, maybe you're just repeating that same behavior or simply struggling to do the opposite of what you've done before, thinking it'll work better than the last time.

Most examples from life and society aren't always the brightest examples of personal control. From a cultural portrait, being a spouse seems like a rough life—we're prone to divorce, fights, sexual temptation, and it seems like faith-based behavior takes a back seat to personal preference. We're not knocking husbands or wives, but let's take an honest look at the big picture. Navigating a marriage of integrity can be a dirty word in today's world because it has a negative association with being boring and dull.

Navigation helps us steer clear of the external distractions while gaining a perspective on internal stressors that pull our stance off balance. When you practice navigation, it allows your spouse to feel secure, which increases trust and affection. That often increases intimacy, i.e. sex. God designed sex to be pleasurable for the married couple. God isn't a prude when it comes to the marriage bed, but He expects that it is not defiled.

Let marriage be held in honor among all, and let the marriage bed be undefiled, for God will judge the sexually immoral and adulterous.

Hebrews 13:4

When we begin to lose control of what is right and honorable within the parameters of a strong marriage, temptations seep in that lead spouses to set their sights elsewhere. This obviously has the potential to lead to emotional and physical affairs. In this corrupted environment, there is no marital accountability because we've allowed our navigation to run without a rudder until we're run aground on the rocky shores of sin and temptation. We'd like to share a few ways to promote personal navigation through an atmosphere of accountability:

1. Think before saying and doing.

2. Own your mistakes.

3. Consider decisions and consequences.

4. Pray God's grace in resisting sin.

5. Confess, repent, and restore.

6. Promise that divorce is never an option and mean it.

Exercising navigation simply means taking the time to step back and gain an objective perspective toward your relationship. What areas can be improved, eliminated, and confessed for healing and new growth? Keeping an even keel based on thought-through decisions creates a protective barrier around your relationship. Practicing personal restraint safeguards you and your spouse from the effects of malicious attacks.

Stone 5—EFFORT

Effort has so many applications in marriage that it's almost impossible to define, but it does indeed apply. Too little and one spouse feels under appreciated, while too much can become overbearing and dominating. A failure to balance effort is often the cause for conflict. Arguments with our spouse don't just happen. There's a process that has begun before that first angry word and foot stomp. Too often we find ourselves at each other's throats without even understanding why. How often have you two argued and an hour later all you can recall is that you're mad, but not sure why?

Emotions that have roiled up until exploding had to have been ignited through a process. This is where understanding marital effort is important for ensuring there is no over- or under reaction from either of you. Women usually expose too much effort through acts of independence, while husbands usually show too little effort through passivity. Let's find the balance.

Has there been an effort imbalance in the marriage, or maybe an absence from both parties while focus has been levied elsewhere? Next, the argument can't start itself. It requires effort. What type of effort is in your relationship? Has it been brewing for a long time, or was it something that flashed hot and angry over an unresolved issue?

There are so many ways to defuse fight-ensuing efforts, but the key is to accept your personal responsibility in creating adversarial environments. Here are a few ways to practice marital effort control.

Contain—Make sure you don't increase the intensity or

allow the situation to branch out of control. Focus on the facts as they are and take the time to completely understand what the issue is about before launching into an attack or unjustified defense on an unrelated topic.

Control—Remove emotions from running the show. Understand that love is not an emotion. It is a choice. With this foundation, make sure that you choose to respond with facts. Facts can include the reality that you're experiencing tense emotions such as hurt, anger, despair, but don't allow them to drive your reaction.

De-escalate—Your spouse is your partner, and not some casual encounter. It's easy to ramp up the intensity for the sake of dominating an argument, but if you "win," you lose. Practicing effort control to avoid high emotional conflict will result in a more productive disagreement and promises to resolve the conflict quicker with both of you feeling better about resolution.

A soft answer turneth away wrath: but grievous words stir up anger.

Proverbs 15:1

3

HER VIEW / HIS VIEW

If you'd asked us about satisfying our biggest needs in marriage years ago, I would've said something about sex or money. Most men would reply with something similar—sex, money, friends, a big party at their wedding, or job security.

What if we told you none those things are even close? As a matter of fact, most of those things drive us in the opposite direction from what is the most important thing in marriage. Here's the truth, your personal relationship with God is the single most important issue in your marriage.

God didn't create marriage for bridal showers and bachelor parties, but to share a covenant relationship together. Since He created marriage for relationship, wouldn't you think relationship would be the most important thing in your marriage? Sure, it is. But the marriage covenant is only successful when it honors God's plan and includes His presence in your relationship.

The reason we've focused on your relationship with God is that without Him, you're going to place the burden of your satisfaction completely upon your spouse. The same goes for them in their relationship with God. No matter how amazing you or your spouse may be, neither of you will ever be God. What happens when you become unhappy in your relationship and begin to doubt that they are the right one for you?

If we fail to set God at the tip of the spear, we're going to become unsatisfied with our loved one, no matter how fantastic they actually are. Unmet expectations are a main cause of divorce. Can you imagine expecting God, and having your spouse try to fill that role? It's not fair to them and it sure isn't biblical.

And then the cycle starts. You get disappointed by that person for not being perfect, so you move on to the next one, and the next one, and the next one. The grass is never greener.

We all have an innate desire to know God, even if we don't have a close connection to Him. It's implanted in our spiritual DNA. Most of us spend time searching for satisfaction from others. We're all imperfect people and will always disappoint each other at some point. This is because we unfairly elevate people as our god (lower case *g*) in place of connecting first with God the Father. This is where unmet expectations occur, which in marriage, lead to divorce. Placing God first causes your marriage to last.

Her Needs

We're going to state the obvious—men and women are different. You're probably thinking, "Duh," at this point, but sometimes, especially in this day of social equality, gender fluidity and attacking masculinity, we tend to forget something so basic.

Just because men and women are different, doesn't mean we aren't equal. We are. The meshing of these two truths has given rise to conflict and confusion from the very beginning. We think the jumping-off point is caused by the second chapter of Genesis when man is formed before woman. Although that might mean seniority gets preference in work life, it's not the same in marital life.

Let's back up to the first chapter of Genesis to understand just how equal man and woman are by perfect design. God didn't fashion Adam to resemble Him, and then toss in Eve as an afterthought. The word *Adam* in Hebrew means man, or mankind. When God refers to creating man in His image, He is saying the creation of mankind. There are two genders in the creation that make up mankind—male and female.

Walking this through, God created mankind, which was man and woman. God's holy hierarchy (chain of command) sets man as the spiritual head of the household. Not as boss, but as servant leader. Woman was created from man (from one became two) to show that once they marry into a covenant relationship with each other as we have with God, the two become one. Both equal, but very different.

So God created man in His own image; in the image of God He created him; male and female He created them.

Genesis 1:27

Part of that difference involves the way each gender internalizes external forces, and the way they relate to one another. Too often, we spin our wheels trying to change one another, when instead our best efforts would be invested in trying to understand what makes each of us unique and special. The differences were by design to attract us to the opposite sex and complement each other's deficiencies.

Instead of men asking what's wrong with their wives, they should be asking whether they're willing to meet their needs. Women have very different needs than men. It doesn't mean either is right or wrong, but different by heavenly design. There are five basic needs that speak to a woman's heart.

Love

Women need love. So much so, that men are commanded to love their wives.

Husbands, love your wives, just as Christ also loved the church and gave Himself up for her.

Ephesians 5:25

Your wife needs to hear you say, "I love you." Just because you said it once years ago during the wedding doesn't mean she's covered for life. You've got to fill her love tank. Not once, but every day. That's how God made women.

Here are some great ways to fill your wife's love tank:

I love you.

You're beautiful.

You're a great mom.

You can do anything.

I'm so proud of you.

I'm so lucky to have you.

. . .

We'll be the first to say that women are tough, but don't take that for granted. God created women to love and nurture, and you need to recognize that through how you treat her. It's easy to crush your wife's spirit with thoughtless or negative words. Your man-mind is just thinking she's sensitive. Well, yeah! She is!

When you fight, your wife needs to be reassured that you love her and that you're not going anywhere. Those thoughts go through a woman's head. When you speak words of love to your wife, this gives her Security, which is another need that speaks to a woman's heart.

Security

Women speak the language of security. They need to know that there is safe harbor in the storms of life, and that no matter what, you will be there with them and for them. You provide that refuge when you love sacrificially as Christ did.

Another way to shore up her place of refuge is by paying attention to her words so you will understand and anticipate her basic needs. Never make her ask to have her needs met— you must take the lead and it'll pay off in relational dividends beyond belief.

You're probably thinking, "Well, how in the world am I supposed to anticipate her basic needs? I'm not a mind reader." No, you're not, but God did give us some direction. Here are three examples:

Headship

Christ should always be the example of a loving head of the household. Too often men assume it means they get to boss everyone around and dominate their wives. That is absolutely the wrong mindset. We always liked the illustration of the difference between "Go" versus "Let's go."

Man is ordained to be the spiritual head of the family. This is a gender-assigned responsibility from God. Leadership can and should be shared by both of you. Leah is a better money manager while I am a self-described man of action. I'm comfortable and supportive with her taking the lead on finances. You should each encourage the other's special skill sets. Let's face it, there are a lot of spouses having to take the solo lead out of necessity.

She can be a leader in your home without threatening your headship. Embrace this. The two of you will be stronger for it. Let us give you a tip. The next time your wife seems over-whelmed, ask her what you can do to lighten the load. Offer to do whatever it takes to lighten her load. Being the head of the household means active participation—it doesn't mean you come home and plop yourself in front of the TV until you have to go back to work.

Sacrificial headship will guide you in meeting your wife's needs in a loving, responsible, and mentoring manner. Praying together is one of the most effective ways of coming into this posture. We'll leave you with this verse that is a great guide for being there for her.

Husbands, love your wives, just as Christ loved the church and gave himself up for her to make her holy, cleansing her by the washing with water through the word, and to present her to himself as a radiant church, without stain or wrinkle or any other blemish, but holy and blameless. In this same way, husbands ought to love their wives as their own bodies. He who loves his wife loves himself.

Ephesians 5:25–28

Communication

If we opened up and talked in detail and with enthusiasm with our wives like we do with our buds at work or the gym, the divorce rate would be a lot lower. To say that men only give terse, guarded responses is a myth. I've seen guys gossip more than the biggest Chatty Cathy, but our conversations become guarded when certain topics are broached. It's easy to talk about other people, not so easy to talk about ourselves. Especially when it concerns areas of our lives that…wait for it…stir up feelings we haven't processed yet. Your wife wants to know every part of you—the good, the bad, and the ugly. She's your safe place.

Dedicate uninterrupted time to talk. Eliminate all distractions (ahem…cell phone, cell phone, cell phone) and actively listen to what she says. If she asks questions, answer them. Also, whether you feel like it or not, respond with full details. This shows that you value her, which helps make her feel secure.

Nonsexual Touching

Men usually associate physical touching with sex. It's how our brains are wired. She touched me! Time to strip down. Look, I get it. I'm a man's man. There was a time when, if Leah high-fived me in the hallway, I'd start peeling off clothes and running for the bed.

Let's say it together this time—women are different from men. They just don't respond the same way men do. Women are slow cookers and men are microwaves. While touch is important, it shouldn't be seen as a trigger for only sex.

A gentle touch, a hug, shoulder rub, or just holding her in your lap without her having to dodge your hands creates security and intimacy for your wife. That nonsexual intimacy goes a long way toward fanning the flames into something more passionate. But the key to meeting your wife's needs is the love, care, and touch given in steady doses throughout the day.

His Needs

This section is for the women, and husbands are encouraged to follow along. There's an old joke about the difference between the perfect date night for a husband and wife. The wife's perfect night starts with fancy clothes, flowers, and dinner by candlelight, followed by a moonlit stroll before being carried over the threshold and kissed softly. The man's perfect date night is a little different. All he requires is for his wife to show up naked holding a pizza.

Are men that simple? Well, we'd like to think not, but it doesn't mean we need complication for maturation. It also doesn't mean our differences will divide us. We were created on purpose with a spiritual intentionality. In other words, God created those differences to complement each other so that you'd remain in a posture of surrender.

While it may require more than a naked wife and pizza, each spouse is happiest when their needs are being met. Is your husband's dream date the same as yours? This is unselfish love. Focusing on each other's needs instead of our own will put your marriage on track for peace and fulfillment.

God commands men to love their wives. But there's a second part of that verse. He commands women to respect their husbands. These are commandments because it's not the natural inclination of men to love. God gave that characteristic to women. And it's not the natural inclination of women to respect. Thus, He commands us to do what doesn't come naturally. Why'd He do that? So, we'd come to Him for the supernatural ability to do so.

We'll say it again. Women and men are different. One of you needs love and the other respect. Don't try to fill your husband's tank by telling him you love him all day. That's what fills your tank. Your husband is designed to run on respect.

What does respect look like?

I'm proud of you.

You're a good provider.

Thank you for everything you do for this family.

You're amazing at _____.

How was your day?

Can I pray over you?

Because respect is the language men speak, men will move toward the place or person where they feel they're being respected. It may not seem like a big deal to the wife, but when men are criticized for not doing or being unable to do something, they immediately default to failure mode. Husbands know you're just trying to "help" and "nurture," which is what God designed you to do. Men know they can be better, so don't stop trying to nudge him there.

I wasn't overly engaged with the kids when Leah and I married. Sure, I was happy to give orders and assign chores, but attending to their hearts was where I needed to focus. Leah didn't rip on me because she knew that wasn't where I was naturally gifted. Instead, she would encourage me and thank me for being there for the kids. It made me feel respected and appreciated, even though I wasn't comfortable doing it. Soon, it became one of the things I enjoyed taking the lead on, and it gave Leah a great sense of security in seeing how I attended to the little ones on a more intimate, caring level.

Just like you wives, men have basic needs beyond a bass boat and a mega remote control. It's important for men to understand that their needs can't be met by material things or other people. Pursuing the spiritual desire of their heart will give them a satisfaction that bigger, better toys cannot.

Honor

Look how perfect this circle is; we go back to Ephesians 5:22–24. This is the model that works because it is the model God created for us to not only love and honor each other, but to also love and honor Him.

Wives, submit yourselves to your own husbands as you do to the Lord. For the husband is the head of the wife as Christ is the head of the church, his body, of which he is the Savior. Now as the church submits to Christ, so also wives should submit to their husbands in everything.

Ephesians 5:22–24

One of the best ways to honor your husband is to allow him to make mistakes (unless self-destructive). Now, the second part of this is not to criticize him for the mistake. Men like forging a path, and although will rarely admit it, they self-reflect and accept the lessons learned at their own expense and own pace. It's a process.

Sex

Men and women usually have very different sexual needs and drives. "Desire Discrepancy" isn't as serious as it sounds, but it is another fancy way to say you both usually get frisky at different times and respond to different stimulations. Waiting for the moment when you're both in the mood will limit your sex to somewhere between very seldom and never.

Men typically have a higher sex drive than women. That's not always the case, but for most men, that's true. This goes back to unselfish love. We talked about how women are slow cookers and men are microwaves. Women are dealing with jobs, kids, activities, and who knows what else. It's easy to make those things a priority. Sometimes the wife doesn't want to have sex, but the husband still has needs. You must both be willing to meet each other's needs and that includes sexual needs as well.

The wife does not have authority over her own body, but the husband does. And likewise, the husband does not have authority over his own body, but the wife does. Do not deprive one another except with consent for a time, that you may give yourselves to fasting and prayer; and come together again so that Satan does not tempt you because of your lack of self-control.

1 Corinthians 7:4–5

It's important that you both discuss sex, and in particular, each other's expectations and how you can both meet them. When sex is used as a reward or a weapon, only bad things can ever result. Sex was created by God as the seal of His marriage covenant, so enjoy it. A lot.

Friendly Fun

Men seem to toil in conflict more readily than women. Maybe it's encoded into our DNA as was needed to protect and defend the tribes and families from vicious threats. Today, it's likely more about office politics or personal animosities, but men are still engaged with conflict. Yet, they tend to avoid confrontation and resolution at home.

Because of this aversion to conflict, men are more productive when the time spent with their wife remains light and loose. That doesn't mean men don't address serious issues, but men don't do drama well. They open up more as the scenario remains nonaggressive and non-accusatory. Those offensive elements switch men into defense mode, and nothing gets accomplished in that mindset.

I'll admit that while I was single, hearing people say they married their best friend made me cringe. My friends were the brothers on the job, and nothing, not even a wife, could break that bond. Well, it didn't take long after Leah and I married that I realized the big, huge, gigantic differences between work acquaintances and a best friend—his wife.

Leah's got my best interest at heart twenty-four hours a day, seven days a week. And part of that involves moving into each other's worlds to do activities the other may not prefer. Not because we want to, but because we love each other enough to do it anyway.

I used to do hundred-mile bicycle races, and I loved being in the saddle and alone on the road for hours upon hours. Leah doesn't ride bikes (at all), but she booked a four-day trip cycling from San Francisco to Sonoma Valley. She was sore. Very sore. But Leah came into my world because she knew he loved to bike. Along the same lines, Leah loves to go to movies. Being in a movie theater is one of my least favorite things to do, but I go because I'm getting to be part of her world and hang out with my best friend at the same time. It's a win-win situation.

You can and will disagree with your wife, but she is your most important ally, your constant backup, and forever your closest friend.

Domestic Safety

There's nothing like having a comfortable place to come home to. The world is a tough environment, and there's relief in knowing there's something safe on the other side of the front door. Make the home a protected refuge for your family. Home is where the safety and security of the heart is.

Deepest Needs

There sure seem to be a lot of needs between men and women when it comes to marriage. It could almost scare you into surrender. But these needs were planted deep in our hearts by the One who created us. It's done on purpose, so we'll pursue someone other than ourselves. Namely, God and our spouse.

There are three very basic, but spiritual, needs. God designed us to share relationship with Him, and part of a loving, sacrificial union is the willingness to submit to the needs of each other. From the beginning, God sought us to rely upon Him to meet our most vital needs, so we could live a full, joy-centered life of worship and fellowship.

To realize this fulfilled life, we have a base need of love, security, and significance. Adam and Eve enjoyed the complete package, and in addition, they also enjoyed a seamless relationship with God. They didn't need a church, or prayers, or even the Bible. Why? Because they were living the story with God every day in an up-close and personal relationship where there were open communications, friendship, and love.

God trusted man with the whole of His creation—earth. Man was placed there to tend and cultivate the land and every creature. He was given dominion over everything because God created him in His image and loved him enough to trust him.

The problem came for Adam and Eve as it comes for all of us in this life—sin. Once they chose rebellion over loving submission, they were no longer able to have the one-on-one relationship with the Creator. God didn't exile them from the garden for tasting the forbidden fruit. He sent them away to protect them from condemning themselves and all mankind to eternal death (separation from God).

Once they were exiled from paradise, they no longer had the direct connection to God to meet their needs for love, security, and significance. The outward source for satisfying their needs through God became an internalized failure to satisfy themselves apart from Him.

Jesus came as a bridge that leads us back into the garden of Eden. Because of this reconnection to the Father, we again have the opportunity to be filled by the Father instead of our worldly pursuits.

The problem we have is, after thousands of years of doing it our own way, we've become resistant to the notion of surrender.

We don't live in a society that's known for surrendering anything. We want what we want, and we want to keep what's ours. Once we come into a posture of understanding that victory comes through surrendering to Jesus Christ, the potential for having the desire for love, significance, and security satisfied by God becomes a reality.

Are you in self-satisfaction mode? You love each other and you love your life, and as long as you're happy doing what makes you happy, you're cool. Additionally, what else are you pursuing that makes you feel good about you?

By all appearances, it seems as though you've managed to satisfy your deepest needs for love, security, and significance, simply by working hard and watching out mostly for old *numero uno*. Well, you know we can't let that lie linger. Each one of those things can be wiped away in an instant. If you're putting your faith in yourself, then you become your god (lower case *g*). Once you've elevated something above God the Father, it also becomes idolatry.

Your reliance on yourself to provide love, security, and significance will begin to decay. The love for the external gratification will overshadow your love for each other. The security in material items become a burden as expenses pile up and cost of living allowances don't. And your sense of significance in everything based on your own ability will fade. What you both thought was serving your needs, has, is, or will destroy what God intended for you.

Please don't allow fear of relying less on yourself and more on God to stop you from coming into a wonderful relationship with Him. Surrendering to God will indeed draw you both closer to Him and ultimately each other. God's purpose for your life is so important to understand. We all have one. His purpose for your life will fulfill the desires of your heart. Don't worry about what opening yourself up to God's will might look like. He won't lead you to do something that He hasn't prepared you to do.

PART II

4

COMMUNICATION

Let's kick off this chapter with a reminder—men and women are different. We were created different by design, and we will always be different by intention. Part of that difference is reflected in the way we communicate with each other.

I grew up running through the tall sugarcane stalks of south Louisiana. The neighborhood kids and I adopted a dialect of a mash-up of English, creole French, and some Spanish slang to enjoy a secret-coded talk that even our parents didn't understand.

Chances are that you and your spouse have your own language too. Maybe some of it is silent cues, disapproving glances, impatient snorts of exhaled air, or a subtle nod of the chin in affirmation. Leah and I even had tactical communications before heading into family and public events, so we'd know when it was time to ramp up, wrap up, or head out.

But in the daily grind of fleeting hellos and hurried goodbyes, we miss important opportunities for communicating with each other in meaningful ways. This is where the differences between us become obvious and often confrontational.

Rare is the good, solid marriage that isn't grounded in positive communications. Social media is altering the way we communicate. It's not just for kids, because married couples rely on texting when they don't have time to talk, or when they'd rather avoid a face-to-face confrontation. We know a couple that claimed texting helped save their marriage because they used to fight every time they started talking.

We're not sure that's a solid long-term strategy, but chances are it's only prolonging what will soon become a major blowout. When it happens, and it will happen, they'll find themselves without a solid foundation for talking through their issues.

Communicating is how we get to know each other. Think back to when you first met. How many hours did you spend talking with each other, clinging on to every word? It was critical for learning about each other, and mostly it was fun. We're willing to bet that you both used lots of positive talk and active listening so you wouldn't miss a single detail.

So, what happened? You're both still interesting people, and beyond the initial physical attractions, love has become a fixture in the relationship. The difference is you are no longer sharing through communications. Talking about house chores, paying bills, and work doesn't count.

Intimate, vulnerable conversations are what cement marriages. If you both have fallen into a rut of only covering the surface in your conversations, or default to negative and cutting words, please know that you can turn it around.

From the fruit of their mouth a person's stomach is filled;
with the harvest of their lips they are satisfied.
The tongue has the power of life and death,
and those who love it will eat its fruit.
Proverbs 18:20–21

We may not realize the power of each spoken word, but the soul does. It's either uplifted or cut clean to the core. Your spouse is not the enemy or some street-level confrontation. Married couples should not measure individual successes by arguments won and lost. Both lose when arguments become the standard. Forgiveness, affirmation, and understanding will help you avoid the marital autopsy.

Can we take a moment to go back to Proverbs 18:20–21? Sometimes we get in a rush and brush over Bible verses when they're ones we're familiar with. But this is so profound that its implications should stop us in our tracks.

Some people think it's just a metaphor that words hold the power of life and death, but consider the actual, literal reality that someone can pronounce that you physically are allowed to live or be put to death. Not such a metaphor now. In a spiritual realm, the tongue either affirms another with positive words, or the death can be the killing of hope, peace, joy, or love.

Wasted words also have eternal consequences. We think that if couples could witness this holy judgment, there would be fewer negative, hurtful words spoken to each other.

While we're thinking through Proverbs, please review everything you've said to your spouse in the last twenty-four hours. How about the last twelve hours, or more realistically, the last few hours? How would you be judged—condemned or acquitted?

But I tell you that everyone will have to give account on the day of judgment for every empty word they have spoken. For by your words you will be acquitted, and by your words you will be condemned.

Matthew 12:36–37

Just as we learn rules so as to not break them, we too can learn or relearn to speak positive, affirming words to our spouse. When we truly see our spouse in the context of God's foundational laws of marriage: priority, possession, pursuit, and purity—there is no desire to withhold positive communications.

I thought my parents had the perfect marriage. They never fought, were always together, and made themselves available to all seven kids. In my first marriage, the fantasy of never fighting, always being together, and being available to my child was just that—a fantasy. Actually, it became a nightmare, which eventually turned into a divorce.

When Leah and I married, it began again. I just knew I'd made a mistake in marrying Leah because we started to have arguments, weren't available for each other all the time, and there was no way to be everywhere for everyone. It was a dark time. After waiting almost twenty years for God to bless me with a wife, did I misread His will? Of course not.

What I had misread was the reality that my parents did not have a perfect marriage. They had a marriage like anyone who was willing to dig in and stick it out, no matter what came their way. What I had missed in the bliss of youth was that my parents did fight, they were absent, and sometimes the kids didn't get to ball practice on time.

Leah and I quickly came to understand we needed to learn how to fight fair. She is a peacekeeper, and I'm genetically geared toward dominating a situation by force of personality. Honestly, it was and sometimes remains a struggle to put away my police command voice in the heat of an argument with Leah. And if you also have a dominant personality, don't fool yourself into thinking that your spouse knows better than to be afraid or hesitant in how they respond to the things you say and the way you say them.

If you fail to provide your spouse with a safe place to fight, then they'll avoid the ring. Their avoidance doesn't signal your victory or understanding. It means they've been defeated, and that is never a good posture for your partner in this life because you've both lost. To borrow a saying from our friend Pastor Dave Willis, "A husband and wife must function like two wings on the same bird. They must work together in partnership, or the marriage will never get off the ground."

The biggest single change in the way Leah and I spoke to each other was the morning we began praying together. It was a tough road for me to arrive at the place of being able to pray with Leah. I had a faithful and deep prayer life on my own, but the reality was, no one spouse could be completely whole in their prayer life without their other equal half. So, the day I stopped operating at half capacity was the day prayer time changed my life.

"Again I say to you that if two of you agree on earth concerning

anything that they ask, it will be done for them by My Father in heaven. For where two or three are gathered together in My name, I am there in the midst of them."

Matthew 18:19-20 (NKJV)

Praying together was tough for me because I was resistant to being vulnerable in front of Leah. By the way, that is the only way we may come before God. Carrying pride, arrogance, cockiness, or general 'tude to the altar will get us shot down every time.

Praying together will show you the right way to communicate with God, and after all, the relationship with your spouse was mirrored in the way He communicates with us. Therefore, praying together serves as a mentoring session with the ultimate marriage coach.

A bonus to praying together is that we begin to ask forgiveness and apologize to our spouses instead of taking pride in getting the last dig in. When we stop keeping score, and recalling past wounds through hurtful words, we begin treating our spouse like the gift God gave us.

A gentle answer turns away wrath,

but a harsh word stirs up anger.

Proverbs 15:1

Here are a few ways to make sure you both fight fair:

Start your sentences with "I" instead of "You"—"I feel frustrated when we're late" is easier to hear than "You always make us late."

Keep your fighting away from your kids unless you model how to resolve it in front of them.

Stay clear of "character assassination"—don't assign negative labels to each other (e.g. "You're so lazy").

If you need a time-out, take it, but agree on when you'll come back.

Avoid expressing contempt by rolling your eyes or being sarcastic. It's toxic to your relationship.

No Silent Treatments

"Just back off."

I confess that I barked those words at Leah after one of many tough times while on duty. She immediately deflated before my eyes. The exhausted but bright, smiling face, which had worried over me during the extended hours of a homicide investigation, now looked defeated.

I was so exhausted from the hours and gruesomeness of the crime scene that I pushed past her and sat in my regular hardback wooden chair. Thus began one of many silent treatment dances we played when the reality of the job became too real to just be a job.

I knew she'd walked off, but I continued to sit there in full uniform and remained quiet. I soon heard Leah, who rarely sheds a tear, crying in the back room. But I was too numb, and by that time, too agitated. Why didn't she understand I only wanted silence?

It wasn't fair then, and it's not fair now if you're doing this same kind of silent treatment over not wanting to communicate, versus your spouse's need to connect with you. When men are in the mood for sex and their wife just wants to hang out, they feel rejected. So why is it any different when it comes to communication?

Couples must learn to exist in the push-pull world of communicating with precision, yet tailoring conversations to protect confidentiality. It's a balancing act that some master, while others fumble. I tended to lean toward the adage of the less said the better. It's an unacceptable way to withhold yourself from your spouse. This also overlaps into daily life. It becomes the pattern for the duration of your marriage. When difficulties arise, you'll find yourselves unwilling or unable to talk it through. Thanks to the silent treatment on everything from what you want for your birthday to why you no longer want to make love, it will continue to drive your spouse away.

We all have the desire to connect through relationship. Married couples are blessed to have the most important person on this earth as their anchor. This is why of all the people we choose to shut down in front of, our spouse cannot be that person. No way can you share a life, but not a talk. Don't clam up. Just like God, they need to hear what's on your heart and in your head.

Let's get spiritual about this. The devil loves it when you go silent. It's the very same tactic he used to cause the fall of mankind. It was just Adam and Eve in paradise, but we tend to think of Eve being caught alone in the garden when Satan approached her. But check this out:

When the woman saw that the fruit of the tree was good for food and pleasing to the eye, and also desirable for gaining wisdom, she took some and ate it. She also gave some to her husband, who was with her, and he ate it.

Genesis 3:6

Adam was right there! Satan found a way to slip in between

the only two people who have ever experienced a perfect marriage, and he tempted her. But Adam wasn't engaged with his wife through communication. Had he been, he would've run that serpent out of the garden. Instead, there had been silence, and the devil knew it was his time to move. It's easy to get complacent and go through the "routine" of life without checking in on each other. We've all been there, done that. But it's these times of separation and lack of communication where it's easy for the devil to slip in.

What's waiting to invade your relationship?

Refusing to talk with your spouse isn't as much about needing to decompress as you tell yourself. That's an excuse. It's about manipulation, and it can turn into a form of psychological abuse. While you're still in the same home, silence can be one of the cruelest forms of emotional abandonment.

When suspicions arise over anything from finances to affairs, pleading the Fifth only serves you well in court, and might very well end you up there—divorce court. Patterns are easy to establish and very tough to break. One of you setting the tone that silence will be the way to non-handle challenges leaves the ignored spouse with few options for resolving serious issues.

On a few last notes, we are designed for relationships. If one of you goes radio silent and leaves the other one yearning for the relationship for which we were created, it's not uncommon for them to seek satisfaction elsewhere. We're not saying it's right, but we are saying it's common.

Here are a few tactics for dealing with a spouse who pleads the Fifth like a mob boss testifying before Congress:

· If one of you decides you need a time of silence or to decompress, then inform your spouse you need this time, but reassure them that you'll come back around to the conversation later. Your spouse will understand.

· If you're the spouse being shut out, don't respond with threats or agitating gestures.

Understand ahead of time that silence is a control tactic to avoid furthering the topic, scaring you into dropping the subject, or avoiding confession or apology.

· If silence comes at the peak of anger, don't poke the bear on principle. Allow a cooling off before insisting that the conversation resumes.

· Don't wait until the silent treatment begins to know how it will be handled. An ounce of prevention is worth a pound of cure.

· The one thing that neither of you want to do is to accept or convince each other that you're married to the strong silent type. Breaking the silence only takes a little effort and a few words. Usually "I'm sorry" works wonders.

Pillow Talk

I like to go face-to-face when it's time for Leah and I to engage in what we call "spirited fellowship." In case you've never heard that term, that's what we call an argument. But our most intimate and vulnerable talks happen while we're lying shoulder to shoulder in bed.

We think guys are most comfortable talking while they're either doing something, watching something, or pretending to be preoccupied with something. Maybe that's why guys talk while sitting at a bar watching the game on TV. It's a way of being engaged and still disassociated from a posture of vulnerability by having to face emotions from the other person.

As we were prepping this section, Leah laughed when I told her my concept of "pillow talk" was supposed to be sexy and flirtatious and lead to...well, sex. But Leah said, "No way." Apparently, pillow talk isn't sexual. Who knew? Her idea of pillow talk is when you're both lying in bed and just...*gasp*... talk.

So, we agreed to compromise. But the truth is, good communication builds intimacy, and intimacy leads to other things. Yes, even sex. Whether the talk is about something playful or serious, women must never, ever disclose anything shared by their husband.

If a man feels his words are smeared and trust betrayed, that will be the last time he opens up. It's difficult for a man to be vulnerable and share his feelings. Don't betray him by sharing his dreams, goals, struggles, or frustrations with your mom, best girlfriends, or social media.

On the other side of the pillow, a woman's words flow more freely. While she doesn't require you to sign a nondisclosure agreement, every word shared between spouses should always be kept between them.

Now that trust is set as a communication priority, let's talk about the way we talk. Women are more emotion based. Some say that as a bad thing, but its possibly why women live longer than us guys. Feelings and emotions are big influencers in life, and the woman most in touch with hers has a major advantage in expressing herself once she knows there is a safe place to land in the marriage communication model.

While women speak the language of love and security, men speak the language of honor and respect. Both are willing to veer off track just a bit, but the reality is, for each to fully feel equal and accepted as a participant in the pillow talk, each responds to their respective language.

Phrases from you like, "I care, and I'll do whatever it takes," are so important to your wife. Meanwhile, husbands seek affirmation through phrases like, "I believe in you, or I trust you." Simple, sincere encouragements are really important.

No matter what your pillow talk sessions evolve into, please never assume your spouse knows what's on your mind or your heart. Direct lines of communications are vital in the fight for marriage.

Try these tips for successful communication:

1. **Care**—You can't communicate with a person who doesn't care.

Be careful in your body language, countenance, and tone of voice.

Be a good listener.

Give a kind and appropriate response.

2. **Praise**—We have to begin with a positive tone.

We enter into each other's heart with praise (Psalm 100:4).

Say negative things in a positive way. Negativity destroys marriages.

3. **Truth**—Honesty is an essential foundation of intimacy and trust.

We need mercy and truth (Proverbs 3:3).

Speak the truth in love (Ephesians 4:15).

4. **Faith**—Believe that God is able to enforce the truth in your spouse's heart.

Women can change their husbands with actions instead of words.

A gentle and quiet spirit means that you have faith in God and won't try to be the enforcer.

Once you speak the truth in love, pray and believe God for the results.

5. **Surrender**—Decide that your mouth is God's mouth and is dedicated to serving and glorifying Him.

5

FIGHTING FAIR

There is a time to "fight" with your spouse. We'll quickly clarify to avoid contempt or misinterpretation. The idea that a couple will never disagree is absurd. If you're expecting to coexist in bliss where you complete each other's sentences, then you're going to be sadly disappointed. The reality is couples argue and that's okay if you both remain mindful and kind.

Leah and I call it "Fighting Fair." Sure, I can out-argue her and intimidate her into almost any decision I want through pure force of will and stubbornness, but is that how God wants us to care for our spouse? Is that how God treats us?

Leah is a true creative spirit. Her mind functions very differently from my concrete way of seeing things. She'll get the inspiration to rearrange or completely redesign a room in our home. When she tries to share her vision, I have been known to shoot it down as being impractical, irrational, or unwanted before she ever gets out more than a paragraph. It wounds her to the core because creativity is her heart's way of expressing herself, and it's her way of showing the family love through nurturing, design, and beauty.

What I perceive in her sharing a vision for interior design is that she disrespects my wish for saving money because I know it's going to cost more than a can of paint. I allow insecurity to drive what should be an open conversation about what each want out of a space in the house instead of forcing my will over hers.

In those moments, I don't fight fair. And like many men, I'm well versed in verbal jousting. This means I can out-argue, manipulate, or flatly shut down a conversation. If not mindful, husbands can easily do that to their beloved. Even after an apology and asking for forgiveness, they must know their spouse's sweet spirit still carries around the scar.

God says the tongue holds the power of death and life. There's also no coincidence that the very next verse in Proverbs 18 talks about how a man who finds a wife finds a good thing and a blessing from God. This association is coupled together to illustrate how important it is for us to speak power of life over and into each other's lives.

It's also a reminder that men have been blessed with a wonderful gift from God in the spouses. Please remember that the way you treat the gift reflects on how you feel about the gift giver. By caring for your spouse, you honor God.

Death and life are in the power of the tongue,
and those who love it will eat its fruits.
He who finds a wife finds a good thing
and obtains favor from the Lord.

Proverbs 18:21–22

Solid Foundation

Leah and I don't know where you are in terms of your walk of faith. We don't want to make assumptions, because ultimately, that relationship is between you and God. It's important to rely on the only complete source of information for building a rock-solid relationship.

God's Word provides both spiritual and practical advice for couples who have shared sacred vows with each other. Simply attending church will no more save your marriage than sitting in a garage will make you a car. Using these Bible-based marriage principles will lead you into a deeper understanding and relational intimacy.

How do we strengthen the foundations of instability in marriage? By building it on the solid rock of Christ, and not the shifting sands of this world. Take a moment and read this passage from Matthew 7.

Therefore everyone who hears these words of mine and puts them into practice is like a wise man who built his house on the rock. The rain came down, the streams rose, and the winds blew and beat against that house; yet it did not fall, because it had its foundation on the rock. But everyone who hears these words of mine and does not put them into practice is like a foolish man who built his house on sand. The rain came down, the streams rose, and the winds blew and beat against that house, and it fell with a great crash.

Matthew 7:24–27

This verse applies to everything in life. Please allow these simple words to speak to you both. Try substituting the word *house* with *marriage*. Switch out rain, floods, and winds for three things that are attacking your marriage right now.

When you personalize it to your story, it hits home. Jesus is not talking about a house; He's talking about you.

This verse from Matthew 7:24–27, as applied to your life might look like this at one point:

Everyone then who hears these words of mine and does them will be like a wise couple who built their marriage on the rock (Christ). And the job stresses fell, and the sexual temptations came, and the threat of divorce blew and beat on their marriage, but it did not fall, because it had been founded on the rock (Jesus).

We are willing to bet this adapted version reflects many of your own experiences. If not, just add your life story into God's Word and see how it speaks to you. The important message is that we will fail if we depend only on ourselves. We do not have the power to thrive absent of God in an environment created by Him. On the other hand, we will be blessed beyond belief once we stand within His marriage covenant.

Facing the facts while growing your marriage will help you both avoid many of these instability problems. No matter where you are in the relationship, it's always wise to seek help to identify the issues, discuss them, and overcome them. It's never too late to get it right.

6

MONEY

Big Money = Big Problems, No Money = No Problems.

Okay, anyone who believes that, just stop reading right here. Money is right up there with kids and sex for the top three culprits that cause fighting and divorce. Added into the mix of life, and we're talking high stress with high stakes. Not a good combination at all.

White Elephants

We'll share that once Leah and I began to discuss marriage, the white elephant marched destructively around the room. *Money.* I had been a lifelong law enforcement officer. Even at my chief of police's salary, Leah's income as a successful author was considerably more than what I'd ever earned.

You'd think a guy would be jumping for joy to have met a wonderful woman with that kind of earning potential, but the truth was, I struggled. Maybe it was the man mind, or the alpha ego working overtime, but it played a huge part in our earliest troubles. Or should I say, *my* earliest troubles.

It's not uncommon for one spouse to make more than the other. Marrying with or without money isn't about control. It's about submitting to God's model for a relationship based on both people trusting each other with everything they have— sorry, with everything God has given them. In case you didn't know, it *all* belongs to God!

Unfortunately, money is a form of dominance we practice over one another. So, unless you commit to a shared possession in the most biblical sense of two becoming one, don't expect your money to marry happily.

While Leah and I were preparing for marriage, I wanted to show her how much I loved her, and that income had nothing to do with it. So like a dummy, I insisted we sign a prenuptial agreement. I wanted Leah to know she wasn't a supplemental retirement fund. I wanted to do something noble for her.

She was mad as a hornet. We'll explain why in a moment.

One of God's foundational pillars of marriage is the law of partnership. This begins with Adam and Eve and remains the standard today. When Adam and Eve became one flesh, that extended beyond physical sex. Two humans enmeshed into one spiritual, married being. It means that everything you own now also belongs to the other. Let's be real. We like to throw the terms "my" and "mine" around. But the truth is, everything belongs to God. He's blessed us with income, a home, cars, or whatever else we choose to spend *His* money on.

Whether you prosper financially, or just get by paying the bills, you're missing a spiritual blessing by not obeying God's

Word to combine everything into one. Once you choose to marry, there can be no *à la carte* of mixing your lives. It's not realistic to say you'll share the bedroom closet, but not your middle child. No, it's all in. When your money is just dating, it may have the tendency to venture out on its own expenditures, new people, or oppress your spouse.

Chances are you earn different salaries, so there is inequity through separate monies. Relational inequity grinds against God's grain. Remember the importance of Genesis: 2:24—two shall become one—one bank account, one practice of spending and saving, and one in agreement on everything from raises to debt.

You must think in terms of fair, not equal, when it comes to dealing with every situation that requires money. Will you mix your money, or maintain separate bank accounts? While either plan has the potential to work, it's hard to imagine that managing your own bank account wouldn't lend itself to problems.

Unless there are binding legal contracts, wills, heirs, or annuities preventing the comingling of monies, God's will for the union of two people entering a heavenly covenant is for two to become one.

Dave Ramsey's *Financial Peace University* is a lifesaver. We don't say that casually, because it has made all the difference in many marriages. There are other resources available, but you must start by asking the question, "Is our money still dating?"

One of our favorite sayings is that if you don't control your money, your money will control you. It'll also walk off while you're not paying attention. One of the best ways to start practicing disciple stewardship is to tithe from every paycheck. Share ownership of your family's income as an equal partner in its stewardship. This was where Leah's fury was centered when I suggested in the estate planner's office that we sign a prenuptial agreement.

Signing a civil contract instead of focusing on God's marriage covenant wasn't what Leah wanted from me. She wanted my heart to be focused on Christ first and then on her. She was offended, and rightly so. She saw my offer of a prenuptial agreement as an easy out clause. "If this marriage doesn't work out at least we'll get to keep what we brought into it." Yikes. No wonder she was hurt. Financial security isn't going to come from a contract, but through Christ.

Here are some great ways to marry your money. We've added a few potential exceptions based on the "fair, not equal" provision.

1. Combine all money accounts

EXCEPTION—Monies you may have invested, saved for your child's education, elderly care for your parent(s), or other historical investment strategies earmarked for specific interests. For example: expecting one parent to defund their child's college savings account to pay for the new spouse's child isn't fair. It'll only cause division among parents and siblings.

2. Work together on developing monthly budgets

3. Set financial priorities

EXAMPLE—If one spouse has a set retirement, yet the other one wasn't able to dedicate money to a retirement account, make it a joint priority to get that spouse caught up.

Look for other opportunities to establish monetary equity for each spouse.

4. Consult each other before big purchases

5. Create realistic family financial goals

6. Discuss money with children in appropriate contexts

EXAMPLE—Blended kids may include one side being accustomed to a level of financial freedom, while the other side only knew budgets and inabilities to enjoy flexibility. Explaining the shifting financial priority will prepare one side, while assuring the other of fair expectations.

7. Skip the prenuptials

EXCEPTION—Like I said earlier, unless there are extreme extenuating circumstances, don't prioritize legal agreements on how to work it out in case the marriage fails. Go all in and commit to make the relationship last—cash and all.

Remember, if you're in a blended family, there are two other biological parents with or without resources and expectations.

8. Remain flexible

9. Focus on what really matters—1 Timothy 6:10

For the love of money is the root of all evil; and while some have coveted after it, they have erred from the faith and pierced themselves through with many sorrows.

1 Timothy 6:10

Money is only tough to talk about before you decide to start talking about it. Drop the pride and ego before discussing money. It's already a stressful topic, even when there's extra cash brought into the home, so be sensitive. Like learning to ride a bike, the more you do it, the more natural it becomes. Do not hit the brakes on your money's management.

Budgeting

I'm is a saver. I grew up poor, except that I didn't understand what poor meant. My dad was a public-school teacher and coach, and my mom stayed home to raise all seven kids. I had food, clothes, and sugarcane fields to ride my bike through.

As an adult, I was a cop. A married cop. A dad cop. A divorced cop. A child-support-paying cop. A broke cop. I was poor, and in that season following my divorce, I felt it. The cloak of darkness lay over me constantly as I checked and then rechecked my bank account to see whether checks had bounced. It was draining the life out of me.

I met with my parents at a local restaurant one night when they flattened out a napkin on the table. My mom pulled out a ballpoint pen and asked how much money I took home each month. Over the next hour, they sketched out the basics of personal finance and budgeting. It was then that I discovered how they'd pulled it off. I would give anything to have that napkin as a reminder of how simple the basics of budgeting can be.

Budgets are not battle weapons we form for attacking our spouse. Setting budgets are no more than conversations that reflect your values, goals, needs, and dreams. Of course, conversations that never take place do no one any good. Left in silent speculation, each spouse will come to question each other's intentions.

Jesus knew their thoughts and said to them: "Any kingdom divided against itself will be ruined, and a house divided against itself will fall."

Luke 11:17

Money is one of the top three reasons couples fight and divorce. It's usually during the divorce process each of them finally begins to consider the role of money. That's because both are watching it march into their attorneys' pockets.

Let's not do that anymore. It would be such a wonderful accomplishment if we could put divorce attorneys out of business. Don't worry about them, they'll find another way to scrape by! Setting a household budget is vital to the holistic health of your marriage. The stress caused by money is usually a result of failing to control your money. Trust us, if you do not control your cash, your cash will control you.

Taking back control of your money is identifying your money personality. Like we said in the beginning, I'm a saver. Leah is not. There's rarely a sale she can pass up, even if she doesn't need it. Her philosophy is there is someone out there who can use it for that price. Leah is also a generous giver. She loves to buy things for people or give money. Her spending used to drive me nuts, and until we started budgeting, it caused me to worry nonstop until it had affected my health and our relationship.

Something that also helped us when it came to money was understanding our respective money languages. Once I understood Leah has an **Amiable** money language and she understood I have a **Driver** money language, we understood where our hearts were. Understanding your spouse's heart will bring clarity to a lot of areas.

What's your money language?

Driver—Money means success, self-esteem, and security.

Amiable—Money means love by buying and sharing to show affection.

Analytic—Money means strength and keeps away chaos.

Expressive—Money means acceptance and respect as the basis for relationships.

Looking at these types of money languages, you can see how vital each one is for understanding the way we not only think of money, but how it plays an important role in our lives. It's okay if you both practice a different money language because the variance helps balance the budget. Where the differences are agreed upon is within the context of a written budget. Avoid the debt and the fighting by being proactive in discussing money management through a monthly budget. You might even find you have the extra cash to go do something fantastic for each other.

Leah also grew up poor, and her dad used money to control her and her mom. He never gave out more money than they needed, and sometimes not even that. His way of showing dominance over his family was to have them come back to him each time, for everything and anything. But instead of Leah developing a saver's language, she used money to show those she loved that her money was their money.

Money can't buy happiness, but it sure can cost you joy. Now is the time to have serious conversations about immediate spending, medium-range objectives like kids, education, vehicles, vacation, and long-term goals such as retirement, a home, or relocating.

The truth is marriage is good for your finances. There are the tax advantages, of course, but the combination of two revenue streams contributing toward a common goal is much more beneficial than working alone, or digging out of the perpetual debt of divorce, alimony, and child support.

Budgeting creates a balanced environment in your marriage, and it allows you both a secure foundation for pursuing other areas of openness and intimacy. There are plenty of ways to begin the conversation about budgeting.

Unless you both are reading this together, one may initially question the motive for bringing up the issue of money management out of the blue. If so, just hold this book up so your spouse can see the next section:

Hi there,

Your spouse is reading our book and this section talks about budgeting money. Trust us, y'all need to have that talk very soon. Like right now. We care about your marriage and can almost guarantee that money worries are already a source of pain in this relationship.

You will both be better off once you begin to control your money instead of allowing your money to control you. Start off by having this talk about setting a budget. It's going to be okay.

Thanks, and we're praying for you both.

Scott and Leah

Money management can be filled with pitfalls. In addition to the challenge of mismatched spender versus saver philosophies competing for control, there is the bigger issue of spiritual obedience. Now, before you say something about the church not needing your money, we're not here collecting cash for the basket. We want to share several truths about the bigger picture of budgeting.

But seek first his kingdom and his righteousness, and all these things will be given to you as well.

Matthew 6:33

Tithes and offerings aren't about financing some pastor's fancy car. It's about submission and obedience. We also know these terms are contrary to our culture's lifestyle. We're more accustomed to being the one giving and expecting the world to submit. This is where the challenge comes into play, but we will ask that you not allow your current concerns to interfere with an eternal and more meaningful blessing—your marriage.

Failing to manage your money is lacking in a form of stewardship. God does provide, and while we may not think He provides enough after taxes and pension withdrawals, His provision is more than sufficient for what is important in life.

When you neglect honoring Jesus by sharing possession and control of your marriage's money, you place yourself above your spouse in a dominant role and demote God to second place. Before getting started on a budgeting process, pray that Christ is Lord over your finances and that in giving it up to Him to bless, you both will be blessed with management wisdom.

Another big picture risk with lack of or poor budgeting is the tendency to disrespect your spouse's input on decisions regarding money. Avoid being in that situation from the start by including your spouse in every decision concerning money expenditures. It may be a small amount of cash on the purchase, but it's a huge issue of respect that can be gained and given.

Rock-Solid Financial Rescue

The idea of debt can be overwhelming, especially when it feels like you're being buried alive. Believe us, we've been there too. We also know from experience that our life choices often make things like financial planning or debt more difficult.

Get a notepad, or better yet, use debt and budget apps or worksheets to write down every debt you have. Every. Single. One. No matter how big or how small. Take deep breaths while doing this because if you've never tallied every single one of your obligations, you're going to feel very lightheaded, if not physically sick.

Do not panic. The only way to heal from darkness is by shining light on it. This list of debt is going to be your light because you've finally exposed what you've ignored or hidden until a crisis was at hand. Once they're written down, you know exactly what you need to tackle. Pay off the smallest debts first.

What can you cut? It's time to reprioritize and focus on the things that matter. You need a roof over your head, utilities, food, and transportation. Those are the most important things. Pay those bills first every month. Your A+ credit rating isn't going to mean much if you get evicted for not paying the rent.

Do you have a $600 per month car note? Do you have two car notes? Getting out of debt requires sacrifice, and sometimes that means you can't drive the best truck or car. Get rid of those car payments. Trade your vehicles in on something that is completely paid for. Even if it's a junker. It's a temporary fix to get you back on track. You'll have a nicer car again before you know it because this time, you'll have planned and saved for it.

What else can you cut? How about cable? Or expensive phone plans? There was a time in our marriage where we had to get rid of everything but the necessities. Are you getting the best rates for car insurance? Have you even checked to compare? This is an area that can sometimes save you several hundred dollars a year.

Do you eat out while at work? Is restaurant life your way of living? Eating out is one of the biggest areas where we throw money away. It's the same thing with those trips to Starbucks for an extra shot of caffeine when you're on hour eight of a twelve-hour shift. Five dollars a day for coffee adds up to $1,825 a year. That would go a long way in paying down debt.

Make your shopping lists and meals for the week based on what's on sale. Are you paying for a gym membership you rarely or never use? Time to cut it from your expenses. You can jog in your neighborhood for free. What about expensive hobbies like golf? It's a good time to take a break. The golf clubs will still be there when you're out of debt and can afford the tee fees.

Getting out of debt takes determination and a mindset that you're going to win. According to 2017 data, the average American household has more than $137,000 in debt, yet the average household income is only $56,000.

You can do it. We know it's possible because we did it. You'll be surprised where you can find extra money to put toward your debts so you can be 100 percent debt free. Is the money from overtime or bonuses going toward debt or next year's vacation? Vacation is even better when you don't come home broke.

What can you sell? Have a garage sale or sell items on social media marketplaces to bring in some extra cash, and then put that cash toward debt.

It's important to use the budget sheet every month. Don't just fill it out. Follow it. Use the cash you have to live within your means. That means no credit cards to fall back on! And start putting every extra cent you have toward paying off the smallest debts first. We tell you to pay off the smallest debts first because it feels good to succeed quickly. Once you pay off that debt (say, for example, you pay $68 per month on a TV until it's paid off), that money can now go toward your next lowest debt.

We're not saying this is going to be your way of life forever, or that you should never have fun. That's what the budget sheet is for. Fun is a lot more...well...fun if you know exactly what you can spend without the threat of your electricity being cut off. If there's something special you want to do, or a special occasion coming up, just budget for it and stick to it.

Guess what? This really is you and your spouse against the world, and if you don't watch each other's back, the bill collector is going to take it all. But you're both fighters and willing to roll up your sleeves and dig into the fray for as long as it takes to pull yourselves out of the dread of debt.

Please don't ever give up on regaining your financial freedom. The average debt takes almost two years to pay off if you follow the plan to the letter. It may seem impossible, but when you're drawing close to your spouse and taking control of what was a bad situation, you begin to experience a sense of control over the fear of debt. Soon, you're making that last payment and enjoying the new lease on your marriage's financial life. Most importantly, pray about your finances and discuss them openly with your spouse. God will bless your faithfulness.

Give and Bless

Leah and I couldn't make church one weekend because a few of the kids were sick. We sat on the couch watching it online instead. Both of us were still in shock over the insurmountable debt looming over our heads. Guess what the message was about? Giving.

Honestly, that was the last thing I wanted to hear. Really, how in the world would we even scrape two pennies together, much less give an extra offering to the church? I felt a spirit of anger sweep over me, and I jumped up off the couch. Fear was still in my soul, and although we faithfully tithed through the darkest of our debt, I wasn't going to give one penny more. It was fear, but I was allowing it to make me angry and resentful.

Leah lovingly suggested that we stop playing it safe and show our faith in God's promise to provide. We'd stashed away one thousand dollars just in case of an emergency, and she wanted us to give that money as an offering. I was *not* happy. No matter my reaction, it wasn't one I'm proud of.

Leah and I are people who get things done. That means we're capable of making stuff happen no matter what getting it done looks like. We're self-reliant, self-sufficient, and yes, at times, selfish. My pride was preventing me from a major blessing and breakthrough. I knew God's faithful promise and how often He came through for us, but in that moment, I was a prisoner to the fear of letting go of that emergency fund.

The second I began to pray, not about the one thousand dollars, but about why I was so afraid, God began to soften my heart about the message of giving.

We invest in a volatile stock market with hopes of return, scratch off a lottery ticket in hopes of a payout, or feed cash into a slot machine with the expectation of a jackpot. So why are we faithless and fearful about investing in the only 100 percent return on our submission and obedience? God!

This truth will serve you well when faced with debt or major financial decisions: go for God instead of gold in all that you do, and while you're both at it, please understand that debt is often a condition of our faith, and not our finances.

Here are seven poverty pitfalls, and God's Word as evidence:

1. Laziness

I went by the field of the lazy man,
And by the vineyard of the man devoid of understanding;
And there it was, all overgrown with thorns;
Its surface was covered with nettles;
Its stone wall was broken down.

Proverbs 24:30–31

Contrary to popular belief, labor/work isn't punishment from God. You probably work harder than anyone you know, but when facing financial difficulties, we tend to hoard our cash and efforts instead of giving the extra push to work for more opportunity.

2. Oversleeping

Do not love sleep, lest you come to poverty;
Open your eyes, and you will be satisfied with bread.

Proverbs 20:13

We know it takes certain amounts of sleep to remain healthy, but most people are plagued by endless fatigue. Thanks to long shifts, overtime, and meetings that seem to never end, we suffer from a lack of regular rest. It is because of this disruptive work cycle that when we do have free time, it's spent asleep. Beyond normal, healthy recovery sleep, becoming a couch zombie is akin to laziness and yet another poverty pitfall.

3. Stinginess

There is one who scatters, yet increases more;
And there is one who withholds more than is right,
But it leads to poverty.
The generous soul will be made rich,
And he who waters will also be watered himself.

Proverbs 11:24–25

Looking at this verse, we know what it is to be stingy, and it's what we are talking about by giving to get. You will never out-give God.

Anne Frank famously said, "No one has ever become poor by giving."

4. Unteachable Spirit

Poverty and shame will come to him who disdains correction,
But he who regards a rebuke will be honored.

Proverbs 13:18

When God is working on you through the Holy Spirit, please don't become one of the unteachable. Be open and sensitive to His work in your life. There is a blessing just waiting for your attentiveness.

5. Addiction

For the drunkard and the glutton will come to poverty,
And drowsiness will clothe a man with rags.
Proverbs 23:21

Poverty can become an addiction when it has become your marriage's identity. Managing your money includes no allowances for addictions such as alcohol, drugs, pornography, etc. It's not uncommon for people or their spouses to develop compulsive behaviors that are health risks and financially devastating.

Studies show that people who have never smoked are likely to start smoking just to fit in with the other people who smoke. It goes the same for abusing alcohol. Surrendering control of your body and will to external influences shows a lack of discipline and interferes with God's work in your life.

6. Birds of a Feather: Worthless People or Pursuits

He who tills his land will have plenty of bread,
But he who follows frivolity will have poverty enough!
Proverbs 28:19

Show me your friends, and I'll show you your future.

Leah and I began a practice of looking at the people in our lives and making decisions about how much of our time we would give them, if any at all. Now, some people take that as being "un-Christian," selfish, and a whole myriad of not-nice names.

The truth is, we don't care. In our marriage, we must protect the precious time we have together. Be intentional who you decide to gift with your time and attention. Wealth is built over consistent effort and focus. Avoid those who cause you to take your eye off the prize.

7. Greed and Covetousness

A faithful man will abound with blessings,

But he who hastens to be rich will not go unpunished...

A man with an evil eye hastens after riches,

And does not consider that poverty will come upon him.

Proverbs 28:20–22

Like all of God's Word, this is profound. Whether it was listed in the Bible or a business manual, it's solid advice. If your sole focus is making money instead of serving others, your career will languish in dissatisfaction. Pursuing earthly wealth ironically leads to poverty.

Don't allow the fear of finances or a temporary debt to cause you to cut corners or compromise who you are. You and your spouse are one in this, and by coveting money or material things, you instantly relegate your spouse below whatever it is you desire. This violates God's law of priority in placing Him first and your gift of a spouse next. Keep that straight and you'll hit the mark.

For what shall it profit a man, if he shall gain the whole world,

and lose his own soul?

Mark 8:36

We almost forgot. That Sunday I was so upset over the preacher's message about giving above and beyond tithes, things could've gone either way for me. It was the prayers that gave me peace and the insight to understand that clinging on to a thousand dollars wasn't going to get us out of hundreds of thousands of dollars in debt. It was going to be our faith that carried us through.

We gave that money, knowing full well that we had a huge

obligation hanging immediately over our heads. We know you hear these testimonies all the time, so we're a little hesitant to share ours. But that very same week we gave our "safety net," we received three big lump sum payments from the most random and unexpected sources imaginable.

Although the three sums didn't even scratch the surface of our total debt, the exact dollar amount of the three separate sources equaled the precise total of what was pressing upon us to be paid at the time. Faith is taking one step into the dark and trusting God to shine His light just before our foot falls. He lights our path in life, love, and yes, even finances.

7

SEX

What Does God Say?

It's funny because Leah's mother still whispers when she says the word *sex*. It's not like she throws it around all day, but typical of her depression-era generation, that word still holds a naughty connotation that's best left behind closed doors.

Let's face it, sex isn't the easiest thing to talk about unless it's among the guys in the locker room, or thc gals while chatting over a glass of wine. Sex has found itself in a peculiar situation. Although God created it to be enjoyed between a husband and wife, the world has perverted it to the point where we act like the devil holds the deed to it.

Maybe it's the stigma that God created sex or that to really enjoy it, we must keep it a secret. Too often we get caught up on the downside of thinking it can't be fun because God is serious business. Guess what? God created humor too.

God designed us to experience the pleasure of sex. Think

about that for a few seconds. There is no other reason for a clitoris other than for pleasure. I know the world has forced us to believe the lie that married sex is boring. Satan's goal is to pervert all other avenues of the flesh. But the truth is, God is still very much in charge, and you can have the best sex of your life—with your spouse.

So, what does God have to say about sex? I know most people begin to roll their eyes or emotionally check out when the topic is mentioned. But it's really very interesting, and it also gets very sensual.

Let him kiss me with the kisses of his mouth. For your love is better than wine.

Song of Songs 1:2

One thing the Bible is not when it comes to sex, is a list of thou shalt nots. Nowhere in God's Word will you find a list of instructions for the way married people must engage in sexual intimacy. Did you know that we are one of the few species that can mate while looking at each other face-to-face?

Go ahead. We'll give you a few moments to think back through the National Geographic episodes you've seen, or a few random pet hookups you might've witnessed while out jogging. Okay, now that you're back, isn't that interesting?

Why did God design it that way?

Because copulation between animals for the purpose of procreation is the mechanical process of replicating their species. Humans, on the other hand, were created in God's image and meant for relationships. One of the strongest bonding agents for a relationship is sex and the physiological effects of engaging in it.

The eyes are truly the windows to the soul. What better way to relate one-to-one than through soul-deep stares while reaffirming your marriage covenant through sex?

Marriage is not a civil contract. It's a Bible-based covenant between you, your spouse, and God. Covenants are not entered into to be broken, and they also require a seal. Sex is the covenant seal of marriage. Or, as Leah likes to call it, the "sticky glue" that keeps us together.

Now that we've agreed there is much more to married sex than the missionary position with the lights off, let's take a look at key Scriptures regarding sex. While God created it to be pleasing to the husband and wife, there must be safeguards in place to protect anything of value. Scripture provides for those protective boundaries.

Breaking those boundaries has consequences. The offense is sin, and the consequence is separation from God. What are the tangible consequences of sex beyond the marriage boundary? Divorce, depression, disease, abortion, and suicide to roll off a few of the big ones. Then there's children born out of wedlock; child support; alimony; counseling; attorneys; loss of respect, career, and social status once friends begin taking sides.

Not to be a downer, but any of these, and so many more, terrible scenarios are possible just because of what? A flirt, a smile, boredom, or a proposition while working out at the gym. Were the clandestine moments of an adulterous affair worth the lifetime of consequences for breaking the holy vow sworn before your spouse and before God?

Let's look at a key Scripture, and you tell me what you think God is trying to tell us. The sanctity of marriage is affirmed in

Hebrews with a very straightforward and powerful word about sex and sin.

Marriage is to be honored by all, and husbands and wives must be faithful to each other. God will judge those who are immoral and those who commit adultery.

Hebrews 13:4

We're not sure about you, but as far as marital sex advice goes, it doesn't get much better or simpler than that. The words that jump out at us are Honor—Faithful—Judge. If we're willing to lay our life down for each other as a married couple, then why can't we lay down our temptations against sexual sin?

Sexual sin didn't start in the 1960s era of free love. Mankind has struggled with it from the very beginning of time. Sex is a frequent topic in both the Old and New Testaments. God knows our need for sex and our weaknesses when sex is involved. He warns us in 1 John 2:16 about being caught up in this world and what our three most destructive threats are.

Lust of the eye.

Lust of the flesh.

Prideful spirit.

Affairs don't start in the bedroom. They start with a glance, and a returned look. A longing gaze at their body and an acknowledgement that it's pleasing to see and a stimulation to the fantasy of thought. Affairs come to fruition because the married offender is conceited with a prideful spirit and is deceived into thinking it's okay this one time, their spouse will never find out, or God will forgive them.

Is living the shady life that important for filling a void in your spirit? If so, there's much more going down than an overactive sex drive. There is no peace in darkness, but there is pleasure in the light of purity and a vibrant, healthy sex life with your spouse.

"Yeah, but it's hard with all that temptation."

It's only hard if you create the circumstances that allow it to become a temptation. The best way to handle it is found in where else? God's Word.

Flee from sexual immorality. All other sins a person commits are outside the body, but whoever sins sexually, sins against their own body.

1 Corinthians 6:18

Connected and committed is the way God intended you to share your life, and your marriage bed. It's so important to understand that Genesis 2:24 is the foundational rock upon which marriage is based.

The process of building your marriage into a bulletproof team does not allow for including others into your sex life. Whether it's the fantasy of another person, the physical presence of another person, or pornography, it violates the core of Genesis. It says the two shall become one. Nowhere in there does it talk about a threesome. It also goes the same for porn. Mental and emotional adultery is just as destructive as physical. When you go outside of the attraction your spouse brings, it's an offense to the gift that God created just for you.

When You're Not in the Mood

Leah and I were at a marriage conference, and the pastor, who we adore, was talking about the joy of sex. Then he began to touch on the truths of sex, and that it's unrealistic to expect both people to be in the mood at the exact same time. He said that he and his wife understood the importance of intimate time together, so when he wanted sex, he'd tell her, "Honey, I want sex."

I tapped Leah on the arm and said, "Honey, I want sex."

She rolled her eyes and patted me on the leg. So much for figuring out how women work. Maybe that's how it works for an old country pastor, but for most of us, there are other paths to be explored. But the truth is, sex, kids, and cash are the top three fight starters for married couples, so let's get to the bottom of it. And just in case what worked for that pastor, also works for you, then disregard what we're about to share and head into the bedroom for some of that good old-fashioned country lovin'.

But seriously, sex is a big deal. It's God's covenant seal for marriage. Even in a hyper-secularized world, some states do not consider marriage legal until it has been consummated. Where did that standard come from? God's Word in Genesis 2:24 of course. The two shall become one. If you find yourself going days, weeks, or even...*gasp*...months, and if you've suffered without sex because one or both of you aren't in the mood, then this lesson is for you.

Remember those days of lying in bed all weekend, making love, and only rolling out of each other's arms when the dog scratched on the door to go outside? What happens to those marathon honeymoon sex sessions? How do we go from "baby love me one more time" to "love is a battlefield"?

Sex is so important that in the very first book of the Bible, God's first instruction to man and woman was to be fruitful and increase in number. We think that's pretty self-explanatory, don't you? Now, if your spouse handed you a wad of cash and said have a great time with friends, there'd be no stopping you, but are you pursuing marital passion with the same vigor as chasing your dreams, your career, or your hobbies?

The problem post-honeymoon isn't so much that neither wants sex but that communication gets crossed when one wants it and the other doesn't. This isn't the time to panic or begin making accusations against each other.

We've mentioned that love is a choice, and not an emotion. While that reality may take some of the allure out of *amore*, it should serve as a reassurance to both of you that neither must worry about falling out of love. You choose to love or not to love; there is no falling where your relationship is concerned. Well, except for falling into bed.

Sex in marriage is too important to not talk about. We talk about it all the time before we're married, so why not when it really matters? It's an old truth that we spend all our time trying to get each other into bed before marriage, and the devil makes sure we stay out of it after we're married.

Desire discrepancy is a fancy way of saying one of you is not in the mood. It happens more often than most couples would think. Actually, over 80 percent of married couples who participated in a sex study reported struggling with one or the other not being in the mood for sex over the month prior to the interview. The same study also reported that desire discrepancy occurred five out of seven days per week throughout the course of the one-month testing period.

It happens because we're human, and life gets in the way. So now that we know there's a cool research term (desire discrepancy) for not being in the mood, we can move forward to handle it like a rock-solid couple should.

A result from the same study showed that spouses who were not in the mood, yet still had sex with their spouse, have stronger tendencies to place the needs of their loved one above those of themselves without an expectation of reciprocation. This isn't tit for tat, it's about doing as God's Word commands.

Do not deprive one another, except perhaps by agreement for a limited time, that you may devote yourselves to prayer; but then come together again, so that Satan may not tempt you because of your lack of self-control.

1 Corinthians 7:5

And to wrap up this train of thought, the spouse who wasn't in the mood, yet had sex just to please their spouse, ended up reaping benefits from the act of having physical intimacy. The physiological effects of chemical responses in the body benefit both spouses regardless of their emotional motives. So not to beat up on emotions, but simply relying on them isn't a good practice or principle for building marital muscle.

And while Leah and I are sure this goes without saying, coercing or forcing your spouse into having sex when they're not up to it does not have the same benefit. So, despite one's desire to give when giving isn't an option, the taker must respect that there are times when receiving does the opposite for bonding the relationship.

Sex is the ultimate way of serving our spouse, and only your spouse can meet that need. Women typically tend to have a lesser sex drive than men, and that's perfectly okay. That's how God made us. But sex is one of the most important priorities of your marriage. We don't care if you must schedule a day and time on the calendar to come together each week, it's worth it. Do you have periods of time where you're short tempered with each other and fighting a lot? When was the last time you had sex? The longer you go without it, the wider the chasm for having intimacy in your marriage.

We know it's hard to do, but instead of waiting to talk until one of you gets angry or rejected, why not do it now. Or right after reading this section or having sex! Here are a few ideas for moving forward when one of you is lagging behind.

Forge Ahead

Marriage is about sacrifice. We give and take because the in-betweens are where the real, deep connections are created in a relationship.

Anticipation

If you're not a fan of spontaneity, then charge up your sexual engine by thinking about having sex with your spouse as you go through the day. Especially for wives, the mind is a big part of sexual preps, so set your mind ablaze, and your body will follow.

Examination

Take time to reflect about why it is that you're not in the mood. Just proclaiming or avoiding it doesn't solve anything. Identify the cause(s) and if one of the reasons is your spouse, then have that mature conversation.

Stoke the Fire

You're both different. Now where have you heard that before? God truly does have a sense of humor. Appeal to each other's needs. This is something ladies need to focus on. I can say that because Leah is standing right here telling me to say that. Women tend to get busy with kids, schedules, work, dinner, and any of the other hundreds of tasks they make look so effortless. But your spouse is your priority. Meet each other's needs. Send sexy texts to each other or set aside time after the kids go to bed instead of zoning out in front of the TV. Get up twenty minutes early or share a shower.

Negotiations

Instead of a flat rejection of no, how about offering alternatives such as specifying another time if they're willing to be patient. Maybe it's after a nap so the headache subsides, or once the kids are asleep so there's no distraction. Anything but a terse no. Rejection hurts. Truth without love is just mean.

The big takeaway from all of this is to talk before one is driven by desire and the other is just driven away. Make sure you both understand that the body's own cycle of physical need may run along different tracks on occasion. That's okay because you're both heading in the same direction together.

What Is Taboo?

Whoever started the myth that married couples can only do the missionary position really needs a kick to the shin. Think back to Adam and Eve. They were the perfect couple. He didn't have a grumpy co-worker to deal with and she didn't have to worry about her friends running them down on Facebook. They were free, and they were naked. Not just from clothing, but in their relationship to each other.

They worked hard managing the garden of Eden, and they hung out with each other with no secrets, no shame, and no sin. They didn't even have mama baby daddy issues. It was truly paradise. On top of that, God Himself hung out with them in the cool of the day to walk and talk.

Can you imagine the most intimate level of relationship and transparency as you and your spouse talk with God? The point we're making is that Adam and Eve were open books before God. Sin had not entered the garden to create the separation between them and God. They were as close as possible, and during that closeness, Adam and Eve were instructed to be fruitful and multiply.

We know everyone is aware of what being fruitful and multiplying means, and to do that also requires something we don't give God the credit for creating—sex. Not to belabor that point, but if we're going to talk about sex, and whether anything is taboo in the course of intercourse, then we need to have a clear understanding that sex isn't some by-product of the naughty things we do in the dark. Making love is as natural as breathing. It's healthy for you and is good for your health. It's not only created by God, but it's encouraged by Him as well.

But like everything valuable, there are boundaries surrounding sex. The caveat is that sex was created for marriage, not casual hookups and booty calls. This is where the dark side distorts the reality of a good thing.

To be clear, we're talking about sex between a man and woman who are married to each other. In this context, the simple answer about what is taboo in sex might surprise you. The answer is...nothing. There is nothing taboo in sex between a husband and wife. Okay, before you start stammering about, "Yeah, but," please put every negative thing you've heard, been told, or thought out of your mind. As long as you both consent, and you're not bringing in a third party, you're good to go.

We work in a world where facts mean guilt or no guilt, so we want to share just the facts as they're presented in God's Word. Nowhere in the Bible will you find a do and don't list for sex between husband and wife. The only stipulation is that both spouses consent to whatever act is exercised.

Of course, this doesn't mean you have to sign off on an agreement before trying something tricky, but part of sharing the blessing of God's gift to the married couple is that you honor each other as you would honor God. If it's mutually pleasing to each of you, then God is pleased. Somehow married people who are struggling have the notion that marital sex is supposed to be boring. That's the reason they are struggling.

We're banking that you've still got questions about this because it almost seems too good to be true. We get the oral sex questions all the time. Again, if you both discuss it, agree to it, and enjoy it, then it's yours as a married couple.

Adam and his wife were both naked, and they felt no shame.

Genesis 2:25

Let's put a red satin bow around this with a huge dose of truth. As wonderful as the reality of sexual freedom is between a husband and wife, it's as equally horrific when sex is taken outside of that boundary. We keep repeating the phrase "sex between the husband and wife" for a reason. Sex outside of the marriage bed is a huge no-no, with just as huge consequences

Marriage should be honored by all, and the marriage bed kept pure, for God will judge the adulterer and all the sexually immoral.

Hebrews 13:4

Like we said earlier, there is nothing off limits to sex within the boundaries of the marriage bed, but there are restrictions. We're also asked about masturbation, sex toys, and pornography. We know masturbation keeps us from giving our whole selves to our spouse, especially if we've satisfied our own needs. But there's nothing to say you can't masturbate during sex with each other. As long as you're pleasing each other.

Everything is permissible, but not everything is beneficial. Everything is permissible—but not everything is constructive. Nobody should seek his own good, but the good of others.

1 Corinthians 10:23–24

Pornography on the other hand, doesn't get off so easy. This is not only a marriage killer, but it destroys your career, your brain, and your life. The devil attacks us in distinctive areas involving lust and pride. It's no different than inviting a third or fourth person into your marriage bed. Do not do that.

For everything in the world—the lust of the flesh, the lust of the eyes, and the pride of life—comes not from the Father but from the world.

1 John 2:16

The only thing God commands is that you stay monogamous, both physically and mentally. The apostle Paul gave some guidelines to the Corinthian church:

But since sexual immorality is occurring, each man should have sexual relations with his own wife, and each woman with her own husband.

1 Corinthians 7:2

This is especially good advice because it's one of the most sexually promiscuous times in our culture's history. Enjoy the no-limits sexual pleasures with your beloved spouse, and gain God's blessing. It'll be the hottest sex you've ever had.

Past Sexual Regrets

"I'm a whore."

Her comment caught me off guard. I never meet with women alone in my office; not even long-time friends. Depending on the situation, I either have a trusted female assistant sit in, or Leah, and Leah was my co-pilot for this particular meeting. I'd known this woman for years. I also knew her husband on a close, personal level.

Before she'd blurted out that declaration, we sat in silence. As you well know, there is never a right way of predicting what someone will talk about when they request a meeting without their spouse present.

Honestly, I laughed a little in my head when the woman said it because what else could she have been doing but joking. Right? She wasn't. She reassured me that she was serious.

She didn't cry, as I thought she might, but she detailed that the pain from her past haunted her. She'd been married for several years, but her husband didn't know anything much about her past. She'd been a single mom when they met, and he loved her. End of story, and no need for going backward to a time before he knew her.

Unfortunately, her husband's unknowing didn't resolve her guilt over a promiscuous past. I'd heard stories through the grapevine, but I was always cautious to avoid getting caught up in salacious talk. It was all too common and fed a daily diet of the rumor mill.

Her past had started to chip away at the wonderful wife and

mother she'd worked so hard to become. She was allowing her past to define her, and that's right where the devil wants us to be. If we're mourning our dark past, we aren't anticipating our glorious future with Christ.

Unless we were born on Monday and married on Tuesday, we all bring baggage to the marriage. Admittedly, some baggage is the size of the Super Dome, while others could be stashed in a penny pocket. Overcoming past sexual experiences requires trust, transparency, and healing. Let's not kid ourselves, promiscuity runs rampant among every community. That goes for men and women.

We believe it's because there is a world of unresolved hurt hidden deep in the souls of people. We carry our pain into everything we do, so no wonder we suffer. Instead of finding safety among friends to put pieces back together, we're force-marched into society's meat grinder of public façades.

But when real healing isn't available because it's frowned upon by those professing to be your closest allies, sex is often used to help hide the hurt. Even if it's a one-night stand where manufactured intimacy is generated, sex is still a powerful form of medicating pain. Unfortunately, it leads to regrettable sexual experiences that follow us into our new relationships.

Truth must be told when trust is gained that your partner will receive it with understanding and no judgment. If you or both of you were survivors of rape or abuse, it affects your relationship's ability to grow into deep intimacy. Sharing your story with your spouse can lead to healing.

Even if the sexual regrets resulted from consensual encounters, the creeping sense of conviction begins to conflict with your attempts to conceal a sordid past. Whether it's a one-night stand or a hundred separate conquests, sex comes with a price. The payment is usually demanded through your silent shame.

Society claims to have liberated sex by freeing it from the marital bedroom and spreading it out in the open. They say married-only sex is repressive and instead, encourage what they've termed "free sex." Well, guess what? Sex isn't free. There's a cost associated with it, and in the context of sex outside of marriage, the cost is called sin. And God is very clear about the wages of sin:

For the wages of sin is death, but the free gift of God is eternal life in Christ Jesus our Lord.

Romans 6:23

Death in this context is separation from God, unless you've contracted a STD that will lead to your actual physical death. Otherwise, it's a separation that means living your life in a spiritual death like Adam and Eve when they were banished from paradise and daily fellowship with God.

In addition to the spiritual cost of sexual sin, the physical debt is a great expense as well. The reason you carry regrets is because sex is like a glue. Now, if it's sex between you and your spouse, that glue is the covenant seal of marriage, and helps ensure the security of that relationship. Sex outside of marriage is a very different sticky situation.

Sex was purposefully intended to be a powerful force for joining two people together in marriage. God's first instruction to His creations was to be fruitful and multiply. The next chapter describes Adam and Eve becoming one flesh. Yes, that means they had sex. How important do you think sex is in the grand scheme of God's design?

We feel the regrets because we've bought into the lie that sex is just physical, and if consensual, there are no obligations. This is a giant lie. Every time we "become one" with someone, whether it's our spouse (Genesis 2:24) or with a prostitute (1 Corinthians 6:16), we imprint ourselves physically and spiritually.

Do you not know that he who unites himself with a prostitute is one with her in body? For it is said, "The two will become one flesh."

1 Corinthians 6:16

In addition to God designing sex to bond us as one flesh through physical intimacy, we're also connected through the release of the pleasure chemical, oxytocin. By complete heavenly design, the chemical is naturally released in significant quantities only three times in a woman's life, and only once for men. Oxytocin is released when a woman gives birth and when she breastfeeds. Both releases are so that a maternal bond is created with the child.

The third time for the woman and the only time a man releases oxytocin is when both are enjoying sexual arousal and release. Oxytocin is what binds us together. It's a beautiful thing between husband and wife. It's not so beautiful when it occurs between unmarried partners because the bonds remain long after the orgasm has passed.

Like my friend who confessed to sex with between fifteen to twenty-something partners, there's a physical, spiritual, and physiological tie that has bound her to every one of them, whether she knew their name or not. And now her husband is connected to all those anonymous men as well.

If you're struggling to break through and experience a deep intimacy with your spouse, but you just can't seem to get past something keeping you back, it's time to examine your sexual history.

Regret comes because of pain, shame, and guilt, but it doesn't mean you're locked into a posture of failure and sexual sin. You can know freedom from the stain of past regrets. Christ Jesus will wash you white as snow, but you've got to make an effort.

The only way to fight the darkness is by exposing it to light. Jesus is that light. You must confess your sins of sexual decadence and ask God to forgive you. Along with forgiveness is repentance, which includes changed behavior.

Bringing your regret into healing should also include sharing with someone else. It must be a trusted believer who will not judge you or intensify the hurt you harbor by amplifying the condemnation.

You are also struggling against the binds of soul ties. These are the unseen spiritual connections that create memories and even fantasies of your past sexual experiences with your partners. You must pray over each of these and speak power over them. You have the supernatural authority to cut every soul tie that has shackled you to the painful past.

We once watched as a pastor took a journal where he'd written out his painful sexual history, prayed over it to break the bonds that tormented him for years, and dropped the journal into a fire. He cut those soul ties by forgiving others, praising God, and releasing himself from the destructive nature of sexual regrets.

I assured our friend that she was not a whore, and I also led her to the truth of Jesus Christ. Kind words are like a bandage on a severed limb. What truly brings healing is the truth of light that repairs the damages done by a life of past sexual sin. The beauty of this is that we know the greatest physician and healer of all—Jesus.

8

FORGIVENESS

Why should we forgive?

The simple answer to why we forgive is because God said so. But if you're like us, saying that does about as much good as being told to eat your veggies. We'd like to take this opportunity to walk you through the process of how priceless forgiving is. And just in case you're wondering what God has to say about forgiving others, let this sink in a bit:

For if you forgive others their trespasses, your heavenly Father will also forgive you, but if you do not forgive others their trespasses, neither will your Father forgive your trespasses.

Matthew 6:14–15

So how does this relate to couples? Well, in this case, forgiving applies to us just the same as it applies to everyone else. It's nonnegotiable, and we can't outwork it or fix it. This is a gift from God, and we'll not, and we repeat, we will not, ever know freedom until we forgive those who have sinned against us.

Forgiving is about freedom. Your freedom, not the offender's freedom. Forgiveness gives you the power to break the chains that bound you into torment, anger, hatred, or the hell of victimization. God gives you the ability to regain the power through surrendering to His command of forgiving. Some see it as weakness, and that's an unfortunate mistake. Forgiving is about power and control you can exercise over your life.

No matter how hopeless or lost you may feel, forgiving those who hurt you gives you strength through Christ. God is very clear that He will forgive you and bless you once you've released yourself from the sin committed against you by another person. You don't even have to say it to the offender. You must, however, speak the words aloud. Go into your private prayer place or take a drive around the block, but God wants to hear your words of forgiveness.

Let's narrow this down to the most important person on this earth—your spouse. They often suffer the most and rarely get the recognition for it. If you've hurt your spouse through neglect, abuse, or adultery, then it's you who must receive forgiveness. If they were the offender, then you must forgive them.

We know it's hard because emotions are in the mix. Pride, ego, control, and often a taste for revenge are all the devil's handiwork. And, because we are human, we can expect to get hurt or hurt each other's feelings every now and then. That's why forgiving is an active process that restores your love connection, security, and intimacy. Give it a shot.

Fighting to Forgive

We don't take the act of forgiving lightly. It might be the most difficult thing we do. We mean, won't ignoring the person have the same effect? We all know the answer to that. No. The stress of carrying around all of that unforgiveness is unbearable and a huge risk to your life, and marriage. Not convinced? Ask your spouse.

Try actively forgiving those who hurt you, and you will see a major difference in the way you develop a spiritual immunity to their jabs and attacks. Trust us, it's not just you feeling the dump truck of life's anxiety. Your spouse and family suffer from it too. How? Because you come home and dump on them. Free yourself and spare those you love by actively forgiving those who harm you.

Forgiving No Matter What

Did you ever unintentionally insult your spouse in public or in front of family? You may not have even realized it, but it didn't take long until everyone else knew what a huge mistake that was. Just because you didn't mean it, didn't mean they weren't left injured. Now, it would be easy to take a stand and refuse to apologize and ask forgiveness because technically you were right, but spiritually you will suffer because of the hardness of your heart against the one you wounded.

The posture of unforgiveness and grudge-holding erupts far beyond the initial offense or misunderstanding. It invades our personal relationships and causes stress for everyone involved. Instead of simply making yourself sensitive to your spouse, you've launched an attack that could grow into a war. Do not hesitate to ask forgiveness in even the smallest things. If your spouse says they are hurt, trust that they are telling the truth no matter how trivial you might think it is.

Too often each partner in a marriage endures injuries that the other isn't even aware of. It's important to stop fighting against forgiving and start rewarding both of you with freedom from strife.

And whenever you stand praying, forgive, if you have anything against anyone, so that your Father also who is in heaven may forgive you your trespasses.

Mark 11:25

It might be a special dinner gone cold, or the errand you forgot to run, but no matter what the act was, once you respond to an emotional prompting, Satan begins to noodle his way into your life. That slimy presence opens the path as temptation slithers in to start planting seeds of doubt, suspicion, or irrational jealousy.

Without forgiving your spouse for the hurts they caused and vice versa, those gaps can destroy your relationship. Of course, we aren't suggesting either of you become a doormat that forgives without confronting the offenses, but unless you first clear your heart of the emotions all tied up inside, the mature conversation meant to clear the air will usually erupt into more upheaval.

Within an atmosphere of forgiveness, comes reconciliation between two. Spirit-led conversations take on an entirely different tone when approached with a slate where unforgiveness no longer exists.

God's instruction to not only forgive, but to bless others goes for your blessings as well. Give it a try, and we know you'll both experience success with communicating instead of steaming over tension-filled silence. Why? Because your spiritual centers are now talking a language of love instead of allowing unsteady emotional accusations to control your marriage.

When you both stop fighting and begin gracing each other with forgiveness, you will be blessed by the love God created marriage to enjoy. Does your marriage reflect this standard for love? If it does, then God bless you. If not, this is why we're working through this book together.

Love is patient, love is kind. It does not envy, it does not boast, it is not proud. It does not dishonor others, it is not self-seeking, it is not easily angered, it keeps no record of wrongs. Love does not delight in evil but rejoices with the truth.

1 Corinthians 13:4–6

PART III

9

THE ABCS OF MARRIAGE

Accountability

Leah's first big book release loomed, and she was unsure what was expected. Actually, writing is her gift. Not marketing. it was way more than she had been prepared to handle. Although she knew little about the process, she immediately surrounded herself with mentors and others to help her navigate the matrix. That book was one of her next forty bestselling books.

I'm what you might call a micromanager. We're not sure if there's a deeper level beyond micro, but if there is, then that's me. I oversaw everything out of fear of making a mistake. But as I gained experience, mentoring, and confidence, accountability looked less like a process for punishment and more like a system of reassurance.

As a couple, it's vital that you both accept an environment of accountability. We're going to talk about the positive angle to it and not the "gotcha" effect. Too much of that and it devolves into judgment of your beloved's behavior.

What is accountability? A few people we know through the ministry used to describe it as ratting yourself out to God. We used to laugh and tell them that would be confession, but they were close. Although we knew the term *ratting out* was more of a joke amongst them, the intention of making known what was done, was absolutely on point.

So then each of us will give an account of himself to God.

Romans 14:12

Accountability is an honest reckoning of self-judgment. Your spouse should also be there to help monitor with an objective perspective, and gentle, encouraging words. The negative connotation comes from disciplinary uses. Back in grade school, in our careers, in civil and criminal codes, and in church, all we've ever known is the reactive nature of being held accountable.

No wonder no one wants to hold themselves accountable. When applied in a negative "gotcha" after the fact, it loses its appeal and application for the sake of what we're working to accomplish.

Let's look at accountability another way.

What if we instead looked at accountability in a positive light? If instead of it being a tool to retro-discover failures, we front-load success by clearly identifying the expectations ahead of time, and then apply accountability measures to progressively monitor and guide the entirety of the marriage journey.

Believe it or not, I'm not, and never will be, a good runner. Especially not a fast runner. Even while training for triathlons and half marathons, my running philosophy is start slow, end slower. But in run training, the timed splits are vital. They are a front-end goal loaded for potential success.

Let's say you are running the mile on a standard high school track. That will be four laps until you collapse into a heap, sucking air in gratitude that it's done. But if you want to set a new record, then you know that there is a goal pace for running each of the four laps.

Running slow around lap two doesn't mean failure, it just means you have two more laps to pick up the pace so that by the checkered flag, you'll have brought yourself back into alignment with victory. Do they wave a checkered flag in running?

I'm not sure because I've has never come close to finishing first, but I hope you get the idea. Accountability is important, and scripturally necessary for keeping our marriage on the path toward obtaining intimacy between each other.

We also achieve our goals more often when we work with someone to help us remain accountable. Not a taskmaster, or judge, or disciplinarian, but in the biblical description of how each spouse is to submit to the other. This is why the "leave and cleave" principle of Genesis 2:24–25 is so important to a marriage. Both are created to complement and support the other as one.

Brothers, if anyone is caught in any transgression, you who are spiritual should restore him in a spirit of gentleness. Keep watch on yourself, lest you too be tempted. Bear one another's burdens, and so fulfill the law of Christ. For if anyone thinks he is something, when he is nothing, he deceives himself. But let each one test his own work, and then his reason to boast will be in himself alone and not in his neighbor. For each will have to bear his own load.

Galatians 6:1–5

We know you might prefer holding yourself accountable as opposed to opening up to your spouse. It's embarrassing to ask for help with a personal problem. It can be downright mortifying to share the details. But God encourages us to not only hold each other accountable, but to also confess our sins to one another for healing. If you can't trust your spouse with every single detail of your life, then you're not receiving the blessing of the two-as-one relationship.

Therefore, confess your sins to one another and pray for one another, that you may be healed. The prayer of a righteous person has great power as it is working.

James 5:16

We need each other. One-on-one, in prayer groups, small groups, online ministry, or the many other opportunities to draw closer to each other. Looking at accountability as a path to marital success speaks to the language you both understand. Coming wide open to your spouse increases their security and leads to greater intimacy. A spouse who knows their loved one doesn't hesitate to share their deepest needs feels genuinely respected and loved.

Boundaries

One of the first things Leah helped me understand in the context of a sound biblical marriage, was boundaries. I was like so many others who focused on work, reputation, and acceptance among peers. I had trouble accepting the reality of being held within boundaries.

Leah had a great way of explaining that you create boundaries to protect what you love, while keeping the threats on the outside. She is correct. Boundaries are meant for our protection. Cells are created for our confinement.

There was only one boundary at the very beginning of creation. Adam and Eve were free to roam the entirety of paradise. Talk about a sweet deal. They were placed in charge of everything God had personally created.

And God blessed them, and God said unto them, "Be fruitful, and multiply, and replenish the earth, and subdue it: and have dominion over the fish of the sea, and over the fowl of the air, and over every living thing that moveth upon the earth."

Genesis 1:28

Except for the one and only boundary, Adam and Eve had nothing to worry about. God made it easy and told Adam to eat from any tree in the garden except the Tree of the Knowledge of Good and Evil. With that one boundary set for everyone's own good, God left them to enjoy the literal fruits of His labor. Well, you know how that worked out, right?

The boundaries you both need to secure your marriage will be different based on your own situation. But those protections must be discussed and very clearly identified. There can be no security in misunderstood boundaries. If there has been a history of infidelity or the potential, then those boundaries might include restricting/blocking access to the third party through social media or the workplace. An issue with over-spending might include boundaries such as budgeting, and both spouses approving any expenditure over a certain dollar amount. They will be as varied as your personalities are, so take time to explore and set meaningful boundaries to protect, not punish.

Will it be a piece of cake knowing there are limits to selfish desires? No, because Satan wants you to cross that line. He can't shove you across it, but he will try to get inside your head to consume your thoughts with nothing else but what's been set outside of your boundary. This is why we want you to under-stand there is security and joy within your own boundaries, and also that Satan is the father of lies.

We're no different than Adam and Eve. We want what we can't have. But there are reasons why we can't have certain "fruits," and of course, there are consequences when we take that bite out of those things that are forbidden.

Following up on the example of Adam and Eve, not only did they violate the boundary and lose their intimate connection with God, but there was another boundary established that they were forbidden to cross. It was the entrance back into the garden of Eden, and this time God ensured it remained beyond their reach with the help of an angel and flaming sword. Yes, some decisions come with greater consequences than others.

How fired up do you think Satan was once he saw Adam and Eve on the outside of paradise and God's will? Yep, the same amount of happiness he feels when we stick a tiptoe across the boundaries of our marriage covenant. What are you doing that brings a smirk to Satan's face?

When we look at the big picture, we're not sure why we are so averse to the idea of boundaries. They are everywhere from speed limits on the highway to the number of calories on a diet. Boundaries shouldn't be seen as limits to our fun, but standard-bearers for achieving success, or simply having a good, safe time.

Where are you in need of boundaries?

Without an objective perspective, you may not see the people closest to you that serve as triggers for breaking boundaries, locations that remind you of "the good old days," or activities that are just waiting to reel you back to your past. We know you might shy away from this topic because it can get uncomfortable to talk about your weaknesses, but unless we do, those weaknesses will soon cause you to crumble. The only hard talks are those we don't have.

Here's to protecting the good stuff.

Seven Tips for Healthy Boundaries

1. Never meet alone with the opposite sex other than your spouse.

2. When you send text messages to someone of the opposite sex (other than your parent), include your spouse on the text.

3. Share ALL passwords. "In marriage, secrets are as dangerous as lies."

4. Don't watch porn or sexually explicit content.

5. Give "side" hugs to people of the opposite sex.

6. Don't engage in ongoing dialogue with people of the opposite sex on social media.

7. Make time together with your spouse a priority.

Consequences

We always tell our kids, "Decisions and Consequences."

As they grew older, they'd laugh and say, "We know, decisions and consequences." Those two words brought almost as much joy as our three favorite words: "I love you."

Decisions and consequences go together, and if there was any other measure by which to use when deciding between one thing or the other, it's invaluable. For us, personally, it was also confirmation that what we probably repeated a thousand times had actually stuck in their heads.

We've purposefully covered what we like to call the Spiritual ABCs over this section. Accountability and Boundaries were explained and encouraged for use in a positive way for promoting marital success. We're going to flip the concept of consequences upside down. Consequences without teeth really offer little support toward the goal of maintaining accountability within boundaries.

Also, the truth is, consequences are usually out of your control. Criminal actions result in consequences handed out by a judge, work violations are handled by a supervisor, and personal indiscretions are addressed by your spouse or other members.

We can't in good conscience water down the importance of

consequences. We face them every day. From waking up late and missing work, to failing to do as your spouse asks and blocking the person who keeps sending suggestive texts. The only upside is that we really hate receiving discipline, so we try harder to remain on the rails to avoid the punishment of consequences.

For the moment all discipline seems painful rather than pleasant, but later it yields the peaceful fruit of righteousness to those who have been trained by it.

Hebrews 12:11

If your relationship has reached the point where the consequences no longer matter, it's time for intensive focus because you're dealing with issues that began much earlier than your marriage. Consequences have no influence when pain is so intense and the need to numb it is so strong that you almost find yourself wanting to get busted in hopes it goes away. We get to a level where we've been hurting for so long that no consequence short of death could make us feel any worse about ourselves.

That's a very dangerous place to fall into. How do we know that there are such serious past pain issues that may be manifesting themselves in problems that are only now hurting your marriage? It's usually when accountability and boundaries are established that these darker issues come to the surface. Please don't allow that to stop you from doing these things. That would be like avoiding the doctor because you got your arm chopped off. Avoiding is not healing.

The problem we face is that we've fought to hide or survive those problems. We've probably hidden them from our spouse, so there's been a resilience developed over the years. Our weakness has been calloused for so long that besides being numb, we also become very hardened. The most hurtful thing becomes the reality that we're trapped in that lifestyle, and no matter how bad we want to do better, to feel better, to be better —we can't.

After the defeat of our spirit and the surrender to living a life controlled by our past pain and current efforts to avoid it, how do we use consequences to our benefit? There are certain influencers that motivate us in everything we do.

There are two ways to best use the concept of consequences, since the reality of them has little bearing in our life, or even death. Consider what our actions do to others. Start with a series of concentric circles. Maybe the outside circle includes your work acquaintances. The next ring holds your friends, while the one inside of that includes extended family. Next would maybe be your kids, and the one after that is your spouse. Of course, the smallest and most affected circle is you.

While you can cross out the innermost circle representing yourself because consequences don't move you to change, how about looking at all the other people in your life who get hurt because you can't pull it together. We'd suggest you draw out this visual. It's stunning when you see that there's more than just you invested in your being able to accept and allow accountability and boundaries to handle deeper issues that consequences can't touch.

The other option for helping the concept of consequences to maintain a sense of value in your life is to understand that the entirety of your life is the consequence of other people failing you. This may be the only way for you to comprehend the bigness of just how important consequences are. We're not trying to lay a guilt trip on you, but we won't give up on helping you to pierce your heart for the reality of cause and effect.

Because your marriage troubles may represent the consequences of someone failing or harming you in the past, your relationship of dysfunction has become your normal. If you bring anything away from this message, please let it be this— you are not responsible for what hurt you in the past, but you are responsible for how you respond to it today. Your marriage depends on you taking steps to right whatever wrongs are causing your marriage harm.

We know this section about consequences got a little dark, but the reality of this is that all of us come into marriage with baggage. While some looks like a small tote bag, others carry shipping containers of it. Unless you both remain transparent about your past and are willing to use scriptural accountability as a positive support mechanism within which protective boundaries are established, then consequences may lead to personal and relational darkness.

Stay in the light of Christ.

Avoiding is Not Winning

Years ago, Leah and I were in a tough spot. We were getting hammered from every angle, including each other. She was worrying about whether I was going to walk out of the door, and I was worrying why she didn't want me to leave. Truth was, neither of us were ever going to give up on each other.

We were in a season of utter darkness. We'd experienced death, loss of family, separation from friends, financial crisis, health threats, continuing custody battles, and our marriage that was built on empty words and lies was imploding before our eyes.

It's funny, but as soon as we typed the phrase "utter darkness," we felt God move to correct that. There was a light that continued to shine throughout that season. Sometimes it was a pinprick, while other times it was blisteringly bright. But the one constant was there was always a light.

One morning while we prayed together, crying out in despair at the latest volley of attacks, the Holy Spirit simply said, "Avoiding is not winning." Now, I'm a sports guy, and I understand that winning takes effort, but I never thought about it as something to avoid or not avoid. What was God saying to us?

Leah has a habit of checking her emails as soon as she gets out of bed. After months of mounting pressure and personal attacks, she finally stopped looking at the hundreds of emails that had piled up in her account. She'd been avoiding them out of fear because of the constant stream of bad news.

Leah was avoiding the realities of our actions, and of course, the consequences that followed. But hiding in a dark corner solves nothing, and God knew it was time to come back into the light.

That day in prayer changed everything. Being accountable in all things is as important as being accountable to each other. Sure, it's hard to worry about anything else while your life and marriage are falling apart, but the reality is, life goes on. We're in a tough society that doesn't allow us the option of avoiding risky scenarios. Your marriage should get the same level of focused attention when it comes to managing risks, prioritizing actions, and giving your most important partner everything you've got.

It will take a while to dig your relationship out from tough times. How long did it take you to sink into them? Consistency is the key. Refusing to avoid the issues that are causing the problems is what God placed on my heart that morning, and it's so important that we share it with you. If it's addiction, don't avoid it. If it's adultery, don't avoid it. If it's financial debt, don't avoid it. If it's unbelief in God, don't avoid it.

There is no perfect marriage, but the best ones come from two people who refuse to avoid, surrender, or fail. You two be those people!

10

TOXIC RELATIONSHIPS

Pruning Toxic People

We used to think it was only the holidays that brought out the worst in people.

The truth is, as a family, you come under constant attack from exes, in-laws, friends, families, community, and sometimes, each other. The levels of toxicity in today's world are what drive us to an early grave.

This is why we want you both to focus on this chapter. If you must read it two or twenty times, do not miss the mark. The people who are toxic in your life, and have leverage in injecting misery, will seldom change their hearts or their motives. We're not talking about the ex who wants to get the kids back an hour early on a school night. We're referring to those people who are shrouded in your misery.

There's a German word, *schadenfreude*, and it helped us to articulate exactly what these types of people are so that we could reclaim power over our marriage. It literally means deriving pleasure from the misfortunes of others. In German, it is "harm-joy." These people sit like crows on a wire waiting to enjoy failure or suffering in others while happily dropping their own poop bombs on your life whenever they can.

The beauty of recognizing this is that you have the spiritual authority to release yourself from them. How do you protect your current spouse, the children you and your ex-spouse share, the children you and your current spouse have, and anyone else in the blended familial mix?

Exes who were toxic during the relationship or marriage don't necessarily remain toxic after divorce. The conditions of a failing marriage may have been the cause of their poor behavior. There are no true red flags that predict or preclude toxic behavior, but there is behavior to remain watchful for that illustrates toxicity.

Prepare yourself and avoid unhealthy confrontations. While your current spouse should be aware of the history and all current issues, your children should not be subjected to an unhealthy or potentially unsafe environment.

Exes are a source of marital strife and eventual divorce if the external influence isn't handled effectively. Marriage counselors share that portion of counseling sessions are dedicated to equipping one or both parties with the tools required to resist the toxic ex's manipulation and control tactics.

How to Identify a Toxic Person

This section isn't for everyone. You might be on great terms with your ex, or in-laws and everyone outside of the relationship with your spouse, but here's a few ways to identify problems if your post-relationship terms aren't so great.

Do they have an unrealistic expectation for accessing you and your children at will? Does your phone ring at mealtimes and bedtimes? Or do FaceTime calls become your ex's invasive surveillance mission inside your home?

Setting boundaries is a priority to save your marriage and your sanity. Set scheduled call times and restrict where the kids may sit to FaceTime or Zoom with their other parent. Your child may not realize they're being manipulated, but it's not uncommon for the other parent to use video calling as a tool to interject themselves into your family through their voice over an open speaker or their image displayed to you, your spouse, and the other kids.

"Show me Mommy's or Daddy's new car," may seem innocent, but it may also be yet another way of building ammunition to use in future battles with you. Short of sticking your child inside a broom closet, it's best to limit their roaming capabilities.

Interrogations

The toxic ex has the misconception they are the only one capable of parenting the child. The child's time with you is merely a distraction until baby is back home with the real parent. The ex feels empowered to grill you over the time the child has spent away from them.

It's disguised by acts of interests in activities or time shared but be cautious about what information is revealed. It's not only a tactic used to make you recount your actions, but it's a control mechanism for directing your actions in the future.

Sabotage

We know it's sounding more like a counter-terror operation than a parenting piece, but we're talking about toxic exes who would be just as happy with destroying your current marriage as they would with doubling your child support while cutting your visitation in half.

The toxic ex isn't your acute complainer. They are chronic, strategic, and relentless. Many spouses do not see the manipulative power influencing them or their shared children. Once the current spouse attempts to assist in managing the invasion, they are often met with resistance or resentment. This is the goal of the toxic ex. While they may not want you running back into their arms, they sure don't want you in a healthy new marriage. Beware the saboteur!

Hearts and Minds

Many courts use the boilerplate custody verbiage "Alienation of Affection." This simply means one parent shall not turn the child against the other parent. Remain mindful of what the child says. They are parrots and repeat what they hear.

Active listening helps you to understand what the toxic ex is feeding the child's mind with, and often what words are being used by the ex to describe you to your child.

It's not always the goal of the toxic ex to terminate your rights of custodial visitation. Many exes don't want the added burden of more time or responsibilities associated with childcare as it interferes with their personal, adult time with friends or a new mate.

The goal among most of these manipulators is they want

you to fail in the act of raising the shared child, so you become dependent on the "one true parent"—the toxic ex. It's about exerting control. Control over you.

Damn the Torpedoes

Statistically, more dads take mothers to court over interference in visitation than mothers take dads to court for nonpayment of child support. While that might be deciphered to show men are more prone to initiate court action, it does illustrate that there's a problem on both sides with neither parent abiding by the court's decree relative to custodial visitations.

The toxic ex couldn't care less about what court papers say. They know them back and forth, and only rely upon them when they suit their needs. Seldom do parents rely solely upon a child custody agreement without ever making exceptions or provisions on the fly. While this is usually done with the child's best interest, it's also a trap to be aware of. Ever found yourself muttering, "Yeah, but last time...?"

I'm sure you know as well as I do that seldom will a law enforcement agency get involved in interfering with the civil process concerning child visitation. Officers are called into custody disputes more often than they're called to armed robberies. Most law enforcement agencies will never remove a child from one parent and award to the other parent unless there is a direct court order specifying that action be taken by an officer.

Most men are guilty of blowing off the toxic ex's behavior as no big deal. And burying your head in the sand might work for a while. But it becomes a big problem when you remarry or have new children. If you value the sanctity of your new marriage, or just your own peace of mind, then give this the attention it deserves.

While it's vital to be objective and not label someone as toxic because of their displeasure over you running an hour late, it is critical to monitor the toxic ex's behavior and attempts at destructive tactics. It's more than a once or twice intrusion. If not addressed immediately, it will become the pattern of your life. It also has the destructive power to end your current marriage.

Ten Tips for Coping with the Toxic Ex:

1. Acknowledge your role in the ongoing conflict.

2. Don't try to intimidate the ex. It tarnishes your integrity and always comes back to haunt you.

3. If you must discuss anything with an ex, make sure it's impersonal to avoid excessive conflict.

4. Preplan or write out talking points to guide through typically emotional negotiations.

5. Whenever possible, give a little to get a little. No one wants to walk away empty handed.

6. If the discussion is about shared children, only talk about the shared children.

7. It's natural for kids to become confused or angry with the other biological parent. Do not use this as a wedge to drive them apart. This pendulum swings both ways.

8. Loyalty and loss are hurtful to the kids. Don't make them choose sides.

9. Forgive like Christ on the cross.

10. Even if you have to bite your tongue, be respectful of the ex's authority over the child and their own life.

Toxic In-laws/Family

What is a toxic in-law or family relationship? And does it mean you have to cut them off completely? No, not always, but pruning can also refer to cutting back.

Toxic family relationships are those that display harmful behaviors and poor conflict management. There are few, if any, boundaries. There's also a lack of empathy and privacy. Some situations can become so severe that there are constant conflicts or even aggression.

It's natural for there to be small conflicts or adjustments to new family members while everyone is adjusting to the new dynamic. But if the conflict continues or the environment becomes hostile or manipulative, you're in a toxic scenario.

A toxic relationship is about control and is a habitual condition that extends beyond the purview of the newness of a new family member through marriage. They are chronic, strategic, and relentless in their pursuit for reclaiming control over their family member. It may not be purposeful at first, but once confronted about the hurt they cause, it should stop. If they don't—it's toxic.

You might have already experienced this, but it's not uncommon for a toxic in-law to join forces with the toxic ex. Birds of a feather really do flock together, or maybe more appropriate, misery loves company.

The foundational rock upon which marriage is based looks to the very first marriage covenant between Adam and Eve. It's called the Leave and Cleave Clause.

Therefore shall a man leave his father and his mother, and shall cleave unto his wife: and they shall be one flesh.

Genesis 2:24

God says nothing about parents or in-laws as part of that meshing into one. Just as it would be unnatural for you to include someone else in your marriage, so it goes for your parents and in-laws. Raising your kids is a temporary assignment, but marriage was designed to last forever. This is where it really hits home with practical application.

Your parents have completed their mission of raising you once you've become an adult. Even if you lived in the spare room a few extra years. But now that you've married, you really are an adult and are no longer your parents' or siblings' responsibility.

Sometimes parents have trouble letting go. That is why God said a man shall leave his mother and father... That is an active term, not lingering between being married to your spouse while clinging to Mommy. The fastest way to fail is trying to please everyone. Focus on pleasing your spouse first. Even if you disagree, have that conversation away from an audience and support them in front of others. Always praise in public and confront in private.

Don't give your in-laws tickets to the freak show. Phone calls to family criticizing your spouse empowers family to try and "fix it" or interject. And by fixing it, that also includes taking sides or possibly even suggesting divorce. If you want family out of your marriage, be careful how often you invite them in.

If your in-laws know as much about your relationship as you do, there's a problem between you and your spouse. They shouldn't know each argument, major purchase, child issue, or any other private matter that goes on in the sanctity of your home.

Forgiveness between a husband and wife should become a continuing process. But parents and families tend to hold on to offenses against their loved one. We've seen parents bring up food tabs from the wedding reception twenty years later. In-laws were not part of God's marital covenant. Have your spouse's back by not talking behind it.

What are our obligations to in-laws?

You should always behave in a Christian manner toward them. Even if they don't share your faith or values, you should forgive them when they offend you, pray for them despite your hard feelings, and never blur the lines between what you owe to your spouse versus what you are willing to give to your in-laws.

Honoring your family and your in-laws is one of God's Ten Commandments. It is stated twice in the Old Testament because it's that important.

Honor your father and your mother, so that you may live long in the land the Lord your God is giving you.

Exodus 20:12

And again:

Honor your father and your mother, as the Lord your God has commanded you, so that you may live long and that it may go well with you in the land the Lord your God is giving you.

Deuteronomy 5:16

You must show them patience, kindness, and respect. You don't have to like them, but God commands you to honor them. Honoring doesn't mean becoming their floor mat or punching bag, but it doesn't mean throwing blows either.

Prior to marriage was your opportunity to get to know the in-laws. If the relationship was strained before marriage, there is little expectation it will magically improve. That would've been the time to create a plan for managing the intrusion of toxic in-laws.

If you don't get along, and it's hurting your marriage, setting boundaries may not help the relationship, but it may save your marriage.

What are acceptable limits that allow you to still honor them?

1. You are not required to submit yourself to doing things their way.
2. You are not required to allow them to disrespect or control you, your spouse, or your kids.
3. You are not required to obey their advice or requests.

Sometimes the best way to show honor to your in-laws or parents is to say "No." They may understand you have your own family and priority, or they may be hurt. Either way, your marriage is priority. We live by the apostle Paul's instructions for getting along. Of course, he ends it with, "If it is possible..."

Live in harmony with one another. Do not be proud, but be willing to associate with people of low position. Do not be conceited. Do not repay anyone evil for evil. Be careful to do what is right in the eyes of everyone. If it is possible, as far as it depends on you, live at peace with everyone.

Romans 12:16–18

Boundaries

We're going to talk about boundaries again, because that's how important boundaries are to your marriage. Good fences make good neighbors.

Boundaries are there to protect what is valuable to you and your spouse. Both of you must communicate your **Position Statement** to each side of the family.

A Position Statement is a written guide that lists what you will and will not accept from family members.

Examples:

- Interfering in faith and religious services of children (grandparents have been known to get children baptized without parents' consent).
- Interfering in child-rearing. If kids stay over with family, they should exercise the same practice as when the kids are at home (diet, movies, use of car seats, etc.).
- Giving money to a child in secret to keep from spouse.
- Giving ultimatums (It's either your spouse or your blood).

What if your spouse sides against you? This is a difficult situation. It's hard to break free from parental control, but again there should have been signs before marriage. Also, if the two of you are truly in a covenant marriage, meaning you are both believers and God is the center of your marriage, then scripture should be your guide. Again, read Genesis 2:24.

If there is still disagreement between you and your spouse on these issues:

- Ensure your spouse knows they are your priority.
- Ask if you are their priority.
- Communicate your expectations that your spouse side with you.
- You and your spouse draft the Position Statement. Hold them to it.
- Protect your children from toxic or harmful behavior even if it means your spouse goes to family events alone. (Example: alcoholism, abuse, vulgar language in their home.)
- Pray God resolves the situation.

Signs that your parents or in-laws are toxic and the solutions:

They butt in (limit what they know about your marriage). They're

- mean (honor them but restrict access).
- They pick sides (avoid allowing them into your marriage conflicts).
- They disrespect your time and space (do not respond to messages and limit time in your home).
- They ignore you (talk one-on-one to them so they must pay attention).
- They treat you like a child (let them know you can handle it and thank them for offering).
- They gossip (let them know you heard they were talking about you).
- They expect too much from you (Once you begin jumping through hoops for them, it will never end. Talk with them).

Let's wrap this up by remembering this—putting your spouse first causes your marriage to last.

Choosing Friends Biblically

Who are the people in life that immediately darken your door? We're talking about the kind of people Jesus Christ Himself could've opened the door for them, and they'd gripe because they had to walk around Him.

I had a friend like that once. Someone who I considered my best friend for decades. When I'd called to share that my son had been born, my friend complained because he had to work late. On the rare occasions I confided in him, he'd gripe because he didn't get promoted. He's got some great qualities, but like so many, it's a twenty-four seven gripe fest. I realized I had to prune that relationship so other, healthier, relationships could grow.

It's vital that you carefully select who you're going to invest your life's time with. This goes beyond you, because now your circle must include those who respect your spouse. It's important to surround yourself with positive, affirming, honest people. Culturally, we're the sum of those closest to us.

So, if we walk among those who stir strife and darkness, how do you think that affects you? We believe in this:

"Show me your friends, and I'll show you your future."

Walk with the wise and become wise, for a companion of fools suffers harm.

Proverbs 13:20

Don't hesitate to walk away from people who don't share your values. We want to clarify this statement because it's not meant to be like the mean girls on social media who block people because they don't agree with their opinion. No, this is real life, and if someone is intentionally critical of your marriage, then that person has got to go.

Leah and I learned this from our dear friends, Toni and Casey. They regularly assess who they will allow into their inner circle. That means some people get moved out. Maybe those who got moved out of the inner circle remain acquaintances, or co-workers, but our friends are very intentional about relationships. It's been a great lesson for us, and one we set into practice years ago. Don't be anyone's fool. Choose your friends biblically.

One who has unreliable friends soon comes to ruin,
but there is a friend who sticks closer than a brother.

Proverbs 18:24

Friends Who Add Benefit

Who's got your best interest at heart? This is a question you should regularly ask yourself. It's especially important in today's culture because relationships shift rapidly.

You and your spouse should both be asking what friends have your back. It's a great way to practice active transparency and ensure you're plugged into who each of you will allow into your life as a married couple. These people should always be a solid source of support when faced with making good decisions. They should be consistent in speaking life into your marriage when times get tough, instead of telling you to file for divorce or that there's someone better out there for you. It's important to share with each other who is in your inner circle and who is in your work circle, and whether those two circles intersect.

Who's in your circle? Without rattling off people you work with, or family, list five people who are really true friends. Not an acquaintance. But a friend in whom you'd confide your most trusted secrets. Someone who you'd allow to see you cry, fail, or be at your weakest.

Greater love has no one than this, that someone lay down
his life for his friends.

John 15:13

We wear masks among acquaintances. Although they might

lift your couch on moving day, are they the ones you'd trust with carrying out your funeral plans and the execution of your will? As a rule of thumb: if you don't trust them in death, you should not be trusting them in life.

There's a social theory referred to as "Who's in your five?" It's based on the ideal that we are the composite of the five people closest in our life. But work partners or casual acquaintances have little to no effect because there's a filter in those relationships that prevents their having influence over your life.

In an isolated season of my life, I wouldn't have been able to name two people, much less five, who were actual friends for the sake of Christian companionship and not a job connection.

During our research, we learned that most men have either one or no close friends at all. As social media continues to separate us from the real world of actual, intimate relationships with real people, the number of adults with no friends has risen from 36 percent to almost 54 percent.

Unless you're fresh out of school and in your twenties, your constricting circle becomes defined by accolades, achievements, academics, and your kids. Promotion and rank add an extra loss of connections because it truly is lonely at the top.

Friendships require vulnerability. Without it, there can never be an intimacy between you. This is where the distinction of friends and acquaintances is most profound. The latter have bonds of loyalty, mutual admiration, and even sacrifice, but beyond occupational obligations, the absence of intimacy is where lines are drawn at the job, the gym, or the gang who heads out for after-work happy hour.

For from day to day men came to David to help him, until there was a great army, like an army of God.

1 Chronicles 12:22

Being alone isn't the biblical standard for people. God created us for relationship. With Him, and with each other. Good friends challenge us and call us on the junk in our lives. They care less about our salary and more about our souls.

We know it's tough to reach out to make friends. As we get set in our ways as adults, it becomes even more difficult. But there is value in relationships outside of the job. Isolating ourselves from others doesn't make us special, it makes us alone.

Faithful are the wounds of a friend; profuse are the kisses of an enemy.

Proverbs 27:6

Don't beat yourself up because you can't rattle off five close friends, or even one. It's the cultural norm of isolationism. You're not alone; even the churches are filled with friendless folks just hoping to make a connection that'll breathe life back into them. It's why men's ministries struggle to sustain growth or a core membership. The next time someone offers to grab lunch or a coffee, take them up on it. Add to your five and add to the quality of your life.

Iron sharpens iron; so a man sharpens his friend's countenance.

Proverbs 27:17

11

FOUNDATIONS FOR BLENDING FAMILIES

Leah and I are aware that no resource for marriage would be complete without a section dedicated to blended families. While we wish it wasn't such a necessity, the reality is most families are very nontraditional. We've hosted small groups at our home for married couples, and what we've learned is that the term blended family is so much more expansive than the traditional definition of two people marrying and one or both spouses having kids from a previous relationship.

The nontraditional nuclear family is almost a thing of the past once we consider how personal dynamics affect a marriage. There's your traditional blended family, consisting of two people marrying and combining their kids from another relationship. Then there are those who have kids who have recently married, and now sons- and daughters-in-law become a type of blended family as you're facing new dynamics. Then there's boomerang kids, adoptions, fostering, elderly relatives moving in, and the many other potentials for doing life outside of the tidy box once described as *marriage*. It's a whole new world for blended families.

We always make it a point to emphasize that we are pro-marriage. We love to see those "first-timers" who met and married and got it right the first time. For folks who have experienced divorce and are adding the pressure of blending, this section is for you.

Now that we've got our disclaimer out of the way, let's get into the reality of blended families. The national average shows that 50 percent of the entire US population consists of blended families. Of those remarried couples, they will divorce 60 percent of the time, unless they bring kids along with them into that second marriage. Although we might love those little buggers, blended families fail 70 percent of the time thanks to the stresses of raising other people's children.

Since the data does show how tough blending is on marriage, why do we do it? Most people cite hope as a main reason they retake the plunge despite the odds. Leah and I want to give you something that most people don't have going into a blended family. We want to give you hope through truth. It's tough, and although we approached blending families with a cautious eye and lots of research, making this life together almost didn't happen.

We are going to throw a truth bomb at you in hopes you'll see that when Leah and I say they should never have made it, you will understand the enormity of the odds they beat. Yes, they say beat and not beating, because they claim victory over the destruction of divorce. Leah and I beat the odds and so can you.

Between our respective divorces, my law enforcement career, a blended family, and a special needs child, statistically, our marriage didn't stand a snowball's chance in Arizona. Not to mention that I carried around so much baggage after twenty-six years in policing, I wasn't a good catch for anyone. Leah only came to understand the effect the job had on me after his retirement as I began to crumble beneath PTSD, addiction, and a life of past abuse that surfaced once the façade's glue came undone.

When Leah and I began to move toward marriage, we decided it was the right time to introduce our children into our relationship. She brought four young kids into the mix. It wasn't a surprise, as we'd been up front from the very beginning, and neither of us would've continued to flirt with the idea of advancing the relationship unless the other fully accepted the "kid factor."

I love kids, but I really loved my own. To say I immediately welcomed and loved Leah's as my own would not be telling the truth. Two of the four were little more than babies. The youngest had just finished potty training. I was forty-eight years old at the time, and they were introduced to me while I was on duty and decked out in a full-blown chief of police uniform, surrounded by other officers in complete alpha cop mode. It was a bit intimidating, if not frightening for a three and four year old.

That first, long weekend saw many crying fits, hiding, and running through other parts of the house to avoid me as they desperately sought the comfort from other siblings and Leah.

We didn't panic or call it a failure. We remained patient and united. What followed were months spent drawing boundaries and erasing battle lines. Losing and gaining trust. High-fiving and avoiding confrontation.

Honestly, I wasn't doing well in the compassion department where little kids were concerned. I was used to my son Max knowing when how I joke and kid around. I can be intimidating, and the truth is, I can also be overbearing. I'd lived alone for almost twenty years, and I liked things my way.

Showing emotion wasn't something I was allowed to express growing up under a dominant father. So naturally, I wasn't skilled or comfortable with the kids' emotional outbursts. My standard response was usually to demand that they stop it. Sometimes it worked, other times they cried more.

I was at a point of telling Leah he couldn't take their crying anymore. I grew up fighting like a vicious animal with his siblings. I played rough sports, I liked to fight, and my career was spent in the most violent assignments of undercover and SWAT. So, when presented with two young boys who preferred video games to footballs, I was at my wits' end.

One morning I prayed God would show me how to be a compassionate father to them, and not a task-driven chief of police. I felt the chains of uncertainty fall from me. The Lord told me I held fear, and that by showing love to these boys, my love for my own boys would be chipped away.

The truth is you cannot run out of giving love. The more you give, the more you have to give. It's like Jesus and the loaves of bread and fish. Love is unconditional, so the supply is unending. It wasn't a matter of sharing a certain measure of love, but the exponential expanding of his capacity to love others.

It wasn't that I prayed for God to toughen up the boys, but instead, I asked God to create in me the man the boys needed. The important point here is to understand that it didn't just happen. The breaking point for those failing blended families usually centers on or involves the children. Here are some tips to do in addition to your prayer life.

Be Realistic—They're kids who have their own parent(s) and just because their parent loves you doesn't mean they'll love you right away.

Accept Loss—Maybe you lost a marriage too and are protective of your own child. Don't forget that your spouse's kids have also suffered greatly through their own family's failure.

United Front—You and your spouse must be united. Kids are like running water—they will find the least resistant path or create one.

Stay Informed—Your spouse's kids aren't just there to be tolerated. They are unique individuals. Get to know and understand what's going on in their life.

New Traditions—We all cling to old family customs but create your own family's memories by starting new traditions.

No Competition—Your spouse's kids are your responsibility—not your competition.

Find Support—Don't bail at the first signs of challenge. If it takes family counseling, do it. It's worth the effort.

Pray for Them—In their presence and in your time, pray for the children in your blended family.

Pray for Change—Ask God to change you. Pray to have the heart of Jesus when it comes to your blended family.

Do Right—Like I was told years ago, "Do right by God" before you try doing right by anyone or thing on this earth. God will take care of the rest.

Leah and I will confess. As we wrote this section, I had to stop the "man" slant and write it neutral. This applies across the board. These are universal truths rooted in God's Word.

Truths in Blending

We have a houseful.

To be honest, summer is probably our favorite time of year. We love having all the kids under one roof for an extended period. It's always a bummer when school starts back up, and along with it, the routine of early mornings, after-school band practice, ballet, karate, gymnastics, and wherever else Leah and I find ourselves taxiing the kids to and from. But summer means long, lazy days filled with family time, swimming, BBQing, and fun outings.

We're very blessed in the blended family department. We've had a few rough patches over the years, but for the most part, our lives and those of all the kids have melded seamlessly. But... there have been rough patches.

We're talking seven kids, five of whom are under eighteen and still live with us, plus the dynamics of Leah and I marrying and creating a new family unit that includes them. Then you have the extended family we created by combining our lives— new grandparents, aunts, uncles, and cousins.

On top of that, the kids have other parents who remarried. Then you add existing children and new children those couples have had together. And then their new grandparents, aunts, uncles, and cousins on that side of the family.

It's no wonder that kids can have a rough transition after their parents' divorce. It throws their entire lives into upheaval and introduces a whole lot of new people at one time. We don't use the word *step* in our family, but it's important to remember that a stepparent is a grief trigger in the flesh. They're a constant reminder to the child that their biological parent is no longer part of the constant picture.

You can imagine the confusion, bitterness, or anger from a child if they're not dealing with a "step" parent situation at all, but live-in boyfriends/girlfriends that could revolve in and out of their lives. Kids have no control over their parents' choices. What they want and need are boundaries and stability.

If you're a blended family, please don't get discouraged if your children (or you and your spouse) are having a difficult time adjusting. Like all great things, it takes time, care, and attention.

From the very beginning, we thought we'd had it made. I spent my career commanding people while accomplishing dangerous and risky missions. How hard could that household of kids be anyway? As we've shared before, family needs engaged parents, not an in-charge chief. What helped us are these seven truths that we developed. Some were stumbled upon by trial and error, and others were intentionally developed to help us stay on track.

1. Priorities

It's going to be important to set your priorities in front of your children from the beginning. God must come first. Your marriage must come second. Your kids come third. Parenting is a temporary assignment. Marriage was designed to last forever.

Children are great at seeing our weak points. If they see chinks in the armor of your marriage, they're going to play you against each other. It's important for them to know that the two of you stand together in all things.

It's easy to get into the habit of putting the kids first. Leah and I were going through old pictures in the garage and we each came across pictures of our kids right after our respective divorces. You can see the sadness and devastation in their eyes, and they're not easy pictures to look at.

When you see that look in their eyes you want to give them whatever you can to make it go away. And it's a completely different dynamic when a new parent comes into the mix. We can tell you from experience this was one of the most challenging things for us, but we also knew it was a necessity. We understood that the kids would adjust quicker with more stability if they knew without a doubt that we were rock solid.

2. Disappointments

There are going to be disappointments. Marriage is a big deal. But maybe your kids don't think so. Or maybe your family doesn't think so. Maybe the ideal picture of The Brady Bunch running through your head isn't what reality is like when you get home from your honeymoon. This is the second or third time around after all, right?

Second marriages can succeed by God's grace, work, and commitment to each other. It's much harder, but we serve an awesome God who loves us, no matter what we've done in the past, and who forgives us, if we're humble enough to confess and ask for that forgiveness.

We found it helpful to be honest with the children about unmet expectations. It's not uncommon for one or more of them to feel cheated with your attention focused on your new marriage. Maybe it's summer camp that's out of the budget this year or they're having to share a room with a sibling. Putting in the work now is the time to make sure that everyone has equity in working through their feelings and expectations. Giving them stability and space to get used to new family dynamics is important.

And as a side note...

When talking about putting the work in at the beginning of your marriage, it's also essential to make sure you and your spouse have alone time at regular intervals so you can connect. But there's only so much alone time you can finagle. That's just parenting life, and it goes with the territory. You'll be empty nesters soon enough.

3. Don't Compare

Don't compare your new marriage, family, life, etc. to the one you had before. It's new territory. It's not a first marriage / first family situation. Don't treat it like one. And don't let your family do it. How many times in your marriage have you heard a family member say, "Well, when he was married to (fill in the blank)...?"

You've both got a past, and it's important you're honest and up front about it. And that you're receptive if your spouse needs to talk about it whenever triggers or issues come up. This goes whether you're a widow/widower or have been divorced. Issues are going to come up. But communication is the key. Not comparison.

4. The Other Parent

Loyalty and loss are important topics to be sensitive to when it comes to the reality that the kids are loyal to their biological parent, and that they will grieve the loss of access to that parent in their daily life.

Don't talk about the other parent in front of your kids. Loyalties run deep with children to their biological parent. It doesn't matter what the other parent did in the past...if they walked out, if they were unfaithful, if they were a deadbeat... whatever their issues. Your child deserves to not have to worry about grown-up issues. That other person is still their parent, and your children love them, even if you don't.

And another thing to remember...there are probably going to be issues come up with the other parent, and you and your spouse are going to have to discuss it. Don't do it in front of the kids.

5. The Ex

Speaking of the other parent...this can sometimes be more challenging than blending your family. If you have a great relationship with your ex and schedules and lives work smoothly, cherish it. Sometimes it takes years to reach this point. That's cool. Everyone is feeling their way in new territory.

The reality is you and your spouse each probably have an ex to deal with. And chances are probably high that at least one of them uses up a lot of your time and energy with drama.

Here's the deal with exes—yes, that other person is the

child's parent. But your spouse and your family that you're blending together are your priority. You've got to have boundaries. Drama from the past and drama from whatever is going on in the ex's life has nothing to do with you or your family. And if they're in a relationship too, it's even less your drama.

There are situations where you'll have an ex text message problems with their new relationship, problems with their own blended family, problems with their finances, problems with work, or problems with wanting more child support. Don't let this become an acceptable practice.

Other than co-parenting a child, this is no longer your life, and anything that doesn't have to do with the child you share together is just them gossiping to you, and potentially "sowing discord" within your new marriage and family.

If the ex is having these kinds of issues, they should be confiding in their new spouse or partner, and you need to put down boundaries, so they know it's not acceptable behavior.

Let us stress how important boundaries are. You might not think they're that important, especially if you've been putting up with certain behaviors while you were single. But boundaries are going to be essential to your spouse. Boundaries give reassurance. They also create intimacy.

When you don't have boundaries, the ex can easily wreak havoc. It makes your spouse worry and wonder why you're afraid to take a stand for your marriage, and whether the past is really in the past. Unfortunately, there are exes out there that will do everything they can to find cracks in your new marriage and sabotage it. Lay out the boundaries early on so this doesn't happen. Stand together. Stand firm. You'd be surprised how many emails we get from people whose spouse's exes are destroying their marriage.

If you're the spouse with the difficult ex, make sure you're including your new spouse in on everything that's going on. Keeping secrets when dealing with a former relationship is just going to bring up worry, doubt, and trust issues. Being up front from the beginning can eliminate these problems.

If you're the spouse who is watching your husband/wife deal with a difficult ex, be patient and remember the two of you are a team. It's sometimes difficult to imagine that your husband/wife could've picked both you and the ex from the same planet, especially if the ex is really difficult or drama prone.

It's very easy to let Satan wedge his way in by using that ex to cause problems in your marriage. Remember, Satan hates marriage. He'll do whatever he can to destroy it. The two of you must do what's best for your marriage and your family. The ex is an adult. They can handle their own problems, choices, and drama without dragging you down the rabbit hole.

The best approach to keeping everything from custody to alimony payments in order is to have legal decrees with everything in writing. Hot button topics such as more child support are easily dictated by each state with a formula based on income. Even if you get along great with an ex, we still recommend having set terms in writing and filed with the court. There could be a day when the ex isn't so friendly and it's a lot harder to negotiate terms at that point. Protect yourself, your spouse, and your family.

6. Schedules Get Crazy!

This we know from experience. When Leah and I married, she had four kids and I had three. Now we have seven. Five of whom live under our roof because they're still young. There are days when we are crazy outnumbered. We really must communicate and have good calendars to make sure everyone gets everywhere they're supposed to be. It's challenging and insane. But we have fun doing it, and I think we've got it down to a pretty good science. At least until school starts again and we have to remember what we were doing.

And look, if we can make schedules work, anyone can make schedules work. Leah and I work an insane number of hours a week (usually in the middle of the night while the kids are sleeping), and we travel a lot (for work). We schedule all of it around the kids' custody schedules, though sometimes we do have to adjust the schedule with the other parents. But it works. Because we put in the time to make it work. You can do it! We promise!

We took our very first trip this year without laptops for an actual vacation and we both survived!

7. You Will Love Your Spouse's Children

It's hard to imagine loving any children like you love your own. But it will happen. If you're putting your priorities in the right order (God, marriage, children), it will happen. You'll worry about their futures, you'll hug them when they're hurt or just need a snuggle, you'll hold them to the same expectations as your biological children, and you'll also discipline them the same way. It might not happen overnight, but it will happen.

Behold, children are a heritage from the Lord, the fruit of the womb a reward. Like arrows in the hand of a warrior are the chil-

dren of one's youth. Blessed is the man who fills his quiver with them! He shall not be put to shame when he speaks with his enemies in the gate.

Psalm 127:3–5

We all make mistakes as parents. But if Christ is the center of your marriage, and you and your spouse make your marriage a priority, your children are going to benefit. Even with divorce in your past, it's possible to start building a godly legacy by the blending of your families.

Parents: It Isn't Impossible

Being a parent to your biological child can be challenging. Being a parent in a blended family can be downright tough.

Your child has known you and your ways since they were born. Blended kids have no base of reference other than you're the new adult in their parent's life. Talk about a tough crowd!

Believe it or not, it's usually the adult who bails on the blended family by giving up on their spouse's child, rather than the other way around. What most stepparents admit to is feeling like they have to compete with the kids for the affection of their new spouse. Guess what? When you marry their parent, the kids are your responsibility, not your competition.

These are five truths I have crafted over my career. They've served me well having moved up the ranks from a rookie patrolman to a city's top cop. Leah and I use them daily as the leaders in our blended household.

1. Never lie to them—This should seem simple, but it's not. Don't lie even about the smallest of things.

2. Never speak harshly to them—Spirit-crushing words rarely heal and are seldom forgotten.
3. Always lead from the front—There's a huge difference in "Go" versus "Let's Go."
4. Be consistent in discipline—No one responds well to wavering behavior that teeters on varying ends of the spectrum.
5. Trust but confirm—You're still in a position of authority and must ensure that they are following the rules.

Focus on finding or creating small scenarios where you can teach the child or children something you know or enjoy. Have patience, and use the moments to build common ground, not to punish them for unfamiliarity.

While it may be easy to boss kids around, practice holding yourself to a higher standard of mentoring. They don't need a job site foreman; they need a decent adult who won't let them down. And who knows, you might end up enjoying them after all.

Everything we do as parents sets a generational chain reaction in motion. Kids of divorce usually become divorced adults. We only know what we know. The good news is, we have the power to break the chains of iniquity that have been passed on to us, not just from our parents or grandparents, but from the very first couple in existence. Once we shatter those generational curses, we pave the way for future generations to know God's love and blessing.

If you had a wonderful relationship with your parents and

their model served as the model you now use in a happy, Christ-centered marriage, then hallelujah. If that's what you're doing and it works, keep on doing it.

But if you're like Leah and I, who have traveled the long route to get to our happy place, it's okay. You also have the spiritual authority to set your path, and the path for your children. Even kids of divorce rebound when their parent(s) shows a remarriage example of a loving, covenant marriage. Whether your folks were Ozzie and Harriet or Ozzy and Sharon, you now set the course from this moment forward. Chart that course wisely.

Mixing Faith and Family

Just when you think you've got it figured out, here comes a doozie. Combining different faiths often makes it impossible. Unless God is in the mix of course! If you haven't yet, now is the perfect time to have this discussion with your spouse, along with the ton of other challenges involved with blending families.

The positive side is that there are generally three options that form the basis of this discussion. One or both of you are:

1. Very God centered.

2. Somewhat God centered.

3. Not God centered.

Don't take this as any shade of judgment, but it's an important part of blended families. The truth is, it's very rare that both partners are at the same place in their spiritual walk at the same time. Seriously, this is the perfect time to really open up.

Leah and I had different paths toward faith. It was each other's understanding and support that gave us the time and space to understand where each other was in our walk with Christ. It was one of the very few things we didn't fight about because it was one of the first things we discussed.

Conversations about faith can get intense, so that's why it's important that ground rules are set before the first defensive response starts to fly. It's not about comparing who is more religious or a better person. That wouldn't be very Christian now, would it? The most common issue we see is that there are different religions involved, and that usually brings various traditions and expectations.

In a realistic way, talk about how tied you each are to your faith. How does each one's faith affect your daily lives in a tangible way? For example, does your religion require certain diets, mandatory prayer throughout the day, numerous holy days, abstinence from certain clothes, activities, birth control, or sexual practices to name a few?

Next, identify areas of flexibility—can Jewish kids partake in Christmas / will a nonbeliever's kids partake in Easter? Your level of commitment to your faith will usually equal your ability to be flexible for the family's sake. If there is no room for flexibility, is it because of being close-minded or that one of you is so devoutly faithful that you just won't bend? We're not suggesting either of you sacrifice your faith, but understand the difference between rituals, traditions, and practicing true faith.

This section can get sensitive, but it's also important to discuss. Another high-risk situation is if one of you is a believer and the other one is not. In the Bible, Paul talked about being unequally yoked with a nonbeliever.

Do not be unequally yoked with unbelievers. For what partner-

ship has righteousness with lawlessness? Or what fellowship has light with darkness?

2 Corinthians 6:14

So, like we said, there is still hope because God provides for the differences.

Let's simplify this with a few well-placed bullet points:

·   Be open to discussing not only what you want, but why faith-based practices are important. Do you have to attend Easter sunrise service because it has deep spiritual value, because it's what you did as a child, or because you want to go early and have the rest of the day free?

·   For both spouses to have an honest talk, each must understand what faith means to them so they can explain it to each other. Sometimes couples realize faith or religion doesn't have that big of an impact in their lives. Should your marriage or kids suffer because one spouse demands doing something without having an attachment to it?

- Faith and depth of spirituality may shift through time. Make sure it is a regular conversation.
- Unless there is some unique court order, most kids follow the religious practice—or lack of religious practice—of the parent who has custody.
- Explain to kids that the other parent does things differently or not at all, but that doesn't make one parent right or wrong.
- Neither parent should force faith or practices upon children and must respect the other parent's beliefs.

Even the atheist should not be demonized for not believing in God.

- Parents must prevent in-laws from meddling— Catholic baptisms by grandparents of non-Catholic children have caused so many serious problems and led to a few arrests for kidnapping and assault (no kidding).
- Parents must agree before having children participate in religious ritualistic acts or "certifications"—taking communion for example, ritualistic cuttings, or water baptism.

Here are a few basic tips to avoid the "religious" rub and ensure that you approach faith in a faithful manner.

1. Have a plan.
2. Agree on how to observe traditions associated with each faith.
3. Share your point of view without being defensive or making unkind remarks about the other's faith, or absence of one.
4. Faith is a "hot button," but this decision is really no different than any other decision you must make when combining families.
5. In custodial matters, accept that whoever has the kid, has the custom.
6. In a blended family, agree to compromise and always refer to #1.

The biblical standard is that God must be placed as the head of your marriage. Your spouse comes next, and kids are third in the faith hierarchy. We know that many parents in a blended family scenario place the kids as priority, but that is a mistake and usually leads to divorce.

Your kids need to see the adults focusing on God, and then each other. They will not be loved any less or feel left out. Kids from divorce often grow up to divorce. But if they have a solid blended family example done right, it reduces their risk of divorcing as an adult.

This is your insurance:

Train up a child in the way he should go,

And when he is old he will not depart from it.

Proverbs 22:6

12

VISIONS OF PROMISED LAND

A Marriage Vision

Fail to plan, plan to fail.

How many times have we heard this and thought we'd just work it out along the way? You are both going to have to roll up your sleeves and get your hands dirty. No marriage is perfect, and the best of them involve two people who refuse to give up on themselves, each other, or their marriage. But just like the best of intentions, there must be a foundational plan. This structure will benefit your marriage when those tough times come. And trust us, they will come.

There's nothing like a good slogan to rally a team or build your business around. This is also true for marriages. Of course, in this case, the slogan is your marriage's vision statement. It doesn't have to be long or complicated, but it does have to dive into the heart of the matter. This is a pretty good one.

But as for me and my household, we will serve the Lord.
Joshua 24:15

Most of us get married and assume once the wedding bash ends, that's also the end of the process. The wedding was just the starter's pistol. You have a lifelong race to run with the best partner you'll ever have. But to run that race with success you must lay out a path.

Too many couples bump throughout each day and figure they'll work it out somehow, someday. Meanwhile, each is growing dissatisfied in their own lives and the relationship. Why? Because no one has identified why it is that you are married and what it is that you both want the marriage to look like. Marriages need a common goal. Why are you married? What's your purpose for being married? Can you answer those questions?

The point is, without purposeful intentionality, you're both only existing as roommates. You have the God-given authority to define who you want to be and what it is that you want to be. Want to be parents? Then write that as your vision statement. Want to travel the world? Then write that as your vision statement. Want to be marriage mentors? Then write that as your vision statement.

No one can want something more for you than you want for yourself. If you don't make the time to develop a marriage vision, or if you don't know what you want for your marriage, it's almost impossible to create something meaningful together.

Once you both invest the time to discuss exactly what kind of life, marriage, and family it is that you desire, you'll be able to create a big-picture vision. Once a unified vision is created, you can begin to create goals and objectives toward achieving that vision. Let's look at this in a concrete way.

Let's say your marriage vision is to have a family:

Objective 1: Have kids—define how many.

Goal 1: Have biological kids—if can't, progress to Goal 2.

Goal 2: Adopt kids.

Goal 3: Blend kids from previous relationships—if either has kids.

Objective 2: Be a stay-at-home parent.

Goal 1: Secure family income.

Consideration 1: Single family income.

Consideration 2: Supplement main income with home-based business.

Consideration 3: Part-time or second job.

Goal 2: Homeschool kids.

Consideration 1: Time and patience.

Consideration 2: Costs of materials and compliance with policies.

Objective 3: Send kids to college.

Goal 1: Open college savings plan.

Goal 2: Choose college prep paths.

Goal 3: Stay informed of changing entrance requirements.

Goal 4: Wave goodbye to kids as they drive off to college.

. . .

Okay, this is just a quick example of creating structure within your vision. But the point is, if you want to start a family, there's much more to it than having sex. Can you do it without a vision? Sure, you can, and please know that this is a structured support system, and not a rigid plan etched in stone.

Your plan will serve like a backbone—strong enough to support the mission, but flexible enough to adapt and adjust. Your vision plan should identify what you both want the marriage to look like. The goals and objectives should be used as that guide for every aspect of accomplishing your vision. There is no fear, limits, or restrictions in a marriage vision, so go ahead and make your relationship the marriage of your dreams.

Dating Your Spouse

Where has the romance gone?

If you've asked yourself that question before, trust us, you're not alone. There's a psychological light switch that changes our mentality about wooing our spouse the second we say, "I do." Why do we stop trying? Our relationship with each other is the reason we married in the first place.

Marriages must be nurtured. Have you ever heard the excuse, "We just grew apart," from one of your divorced friends? If they'd been dating and putting in quality time with each other to nurture their relationship, chances are, they wouldn't be divorced.

Marriage is to be celebrated, not put on a shelf to gather dust as the years pass. One of the biggest mistakes we made in our marriage early on was not taking the time to celebrate our union. We didn't even take time to honeymoon! We just went back to work and the daily grind. Neither of us felt like we'd done anything special, and what a disservice that was to God and the holy covenant we made with Him.

Dating is more important during your marriage than it ever was before you got married. Carving out a special time to spend with your spouse tells them you still love them and that you want to be with them. Yes! You do! We promise. If we can do it with five kids at home and our work schedules, you can do it too. We'll give tips for carving out time in the upcoming pages.

It's okay! You don't need money to connect with your spouse. We're going to give ideas for all different kinds of dates.

The grass is greener where it's watered. What did you talk about before you got married? What made you get that dreamy look in your eyes and stay up until all hours of the night talking? Great communication is key. You might be rusty, but it'll come back like riding a bike.

"I don't have time."

We've been guilty of uttering those words a time or two. I bet you have too. But the truth is, it's not time that's our worst enemy, it's priorities. One of the most important things God did in Genesis was to create Eve, because He didn't want man to be alone.

It is not good that the man should be alone; I will make him a helper fit for him.

Genesis 2:18

Marriage was designed to mirror what our relationship with Christ is supposed to be like. So, after our relationship with Christ, marriage is our next priority. Even before our children. The greatest gift you can give your children is parents that have a healthy marriage. This also means your marriage should come before work, bills, friends, school, and Facebook.

There are nights where we'll put the kids to bed, hop on the Harley, and go get ice cream just so we can spend twenty minutes alone together. If you look for the time, you'll find the time.

Tips for Making Time:

Make your marriage a priority.

Get in sync! Coordinate your calendars.

Schedule at least thirty minutes of alone time (no kids!) where the two of you can check in with each other and see if there are any issues.

If your kids are little and you have trouble finding babysitters, schedule one date night per month. Trade babysitting time with other couples in lieu of spending money.

Make it a goal for date night to become a weekly occurrence. Chances are, when you start to prioritize, you'll be able to find an hour or two for your spouse.

Money and Dating Your Spouse

Is there anything less romantic than a conversation about money? The fact is, money is one of the leading causes of divorce. Date nights to reconnect with your spouse shouldn't be about money, especially if this is a hot button topic for you. Don't break the bank dating your spouse. Adding debt to the problem won't make for an enjoyable date night.

Free Date Night Ideas

- An indoor picnic—spread a blanket in front of the fireplace (even in summer!), open a bottle of wine, and have a light meal and great conversation. Steal a few kisses along the way.
- Movie night—curl up on the couch and snuggle while watching a movie. Popcorn is optional.
- Stargazing—lay a blanket on the ground and look

up at the stars. It's a great time to talk about your dreams for the future.

- Take a scenic bike ride. Extra points if you pack a picnic to take with you.
- Have a pool? Go skinny-dipping!
- Video game night. There's nothing like a competitive game of *Mario Kart* to get the blood pumping. It's fun to be a kid again.
- Go window-shopping. It's fun to dream big together.
- Take a luxury sports car out for a test drive. Have fun!
- The library—if you love to read as much as we do, this is an awesome date.
- Heat things up in the kitchen. Make a romantic dinner for two together.
- During the holiday season, ride around and look at Christmas lights. Bring a thermos of hot chocolate.
- Have a backyard campout. Make a fire and cook s'mores. Pitch a tent and share a sleeping bag.
- Find a scenic location and watch the sunset together.

Other Date Nights

- Painting with a Twist (We love it!).
- Dress up in your finest and eat at a fancy restaurant.
- Go to a soda shop and share a milk- shake with two straws.
- Go ice-skating.

- Charter a boat for a romantic sunset sail.
- Go to a drive-in movie. Sneak kisses when it gets dark.
- Play golf, even if you're bad. Sometimes being bad makes it more fun.
- Recreate your very first date.
- Meet at a coffee shop separately and pretend you're meeting for the first time.
- Go to a wine and cheese tasting.
- Make a date at the shooting range and have a target competition.
- Go to an arcade and be kids again.
- Find a traveling carnival and kiss at the top of the Ferris wheel.
- Get a hotel room and order room service. Wake up to watch the sunrise together.
- Have a couple's spa day and relax.

Communication and Reconnection

Remember when you hung on to their every word? When you'd talk for hours on the phone, or drift off to sleep just as the sun was starting to rise because of great conversation? That connection is still there, but sometimes it's hard to recognize when you have children, or stresses like bills and work.

Maybe it's been so long since you've been on a date together that you feel like two strangers with nothing in common. Here's a few icebreakers to get you going:

1. If you could give your younger self one piece of advice, what would it be?

2. What's the most adventurous thing you've ever done?

3. If money was no object, what's one vacation destination you'd like to go to?

4. What's your favorite memory of our wedding day?

5. How can I pray for you?

6. If you could choose any career, what would it be?

7. How often would you like to have sex?

8. Is there anything you've always wanted to do during sex?

9. What's your best memory with one of your parents?

10. Do I have any of the same qualities as your mother/father?

11. What kind of legacy would you like to leave for our children?

12. What's a song that describes our marriage?

13. What's your most embarrassing moment?

14. What's your favorite movie of all time?

15. Do you have a bucket list? What are some things on it?

Let's Wrap It Up

Remember when you'd walk across glass to get a glimpse of your sweetie? What happened? Don't ever forget what it was that drew you together. In fact, do those things often. The truth is marriage takes time and effort. If you struggle connecting with your spouse, we've been where you are, and we understand that sometimes things seem hopeless.

Making your marriage a priority is the most important thing you can do after having a relationship with Christ. We want to encourage you that, no matter what season of marriage you're in, you can have a blessed, happy, and whole life with your spouse. Dating your spouse again will reopen doors of communication and set you on the path toward success in your marriage.

Here are just a few benefits of being in love:

Physical Changes—Love has physiological effects on your body. Chemical levels, such as dopamine, testosterone, norepinephrine, histocompatibility complex (MHC), and pheromones, shift. These are all positive benefits. Dopamine is the brain's pleasure chemical; oxytocin is the bonding/intimacy chemical. Hugging and kissing are important. Testosterone is in both male and females, though higher in males. It ups your sex drive. Norepinephrine increases arousal and alertness, promotes vigilance, enhances formation and retrieval of memory, and focuses attention.

Perspective—Love shifts your self-centered worldview into a shared, or partner-focused, lens. Learning to see the world through another person's heart is a powerful experience. It becomes a more transparent process as trust and love deepens.

Fighting Clean—Single people fight for one thing—preservation for their way of life. Throw a monkey wrench in their machinery and they come out fighting like an angry cat mistakenly bathed by a toilet's flush. Love softens the heart for considering someone else's point of view, and the potential for understanding that the world really doesn't revolve around you. Example: praying together.

Sexier Sex—Intimacy and trust lead to increased sexual pleasure. While being single and ready to mingle might make for a great beer commercial campaign, the reality of lonely nights, untrustworthy partners, or revolving-door relations eventually leads to sexual dissatisfaction. Monogamy, trust, and transparency stimulate intimacy, which leads to the type of sex God designed for us—marriage bed super sex.

A Better You—Let's face it, when it's only you that you have to please, becoming self-consumed is almost guaranteed. Without outside stimuli, rare is the occasion to grow or improve. Because it is God's expressed will that two people should become one, it's not only pleasing to Him, but immeasurably pleasing to you.

...AND THAT'S NOT ALL

Less Stress—Married people have less dramatic responses to psychological stress.

Richer—Married people experience a net worth of 77 percent more wealth per person than single people. Married people also gain significantly more wealth than divorced people.

Safer—Married people take fewer risks, including substance abuse, and live happier, with better health benefits.

Survive—Better cancer survival rate than single or divorced.

Live Longer—Living with a partner lowers the mortality rate for men by 80 percent and for women by 59 percent. Cohabitation before marriage reduces the lifespan according to statistics.

Happily Ever After

Leah and I always have the hardest time when it comes to the end of a book. It's the same way when we have to say goodbye to people after church. We know they'll be back the next week, but the bonds built through information, sharing, and prayer connect us all to one another. Of course, it should be difficult to close because we've been through so much with you.

But in the same way we always make sure friends leave our home with food, snacks, or at least a plastic cup full of tea, we want to bless you with the truths of why we began this journey with you and what you can expect to find up ahead as you walk together.

Is there such a thing as happily ever after? Yes. You can be sure of this because it was God Himself who created marriage. God has never created anything to fail. Marriage is the way He relates to us, so it is designed to be lasting. How we support it, partake of it, and honor that relationship is up to us.

It's the same way with our marriage. It was designed by God so that we'd care and support one another; enjoy relationship with our suitable mate; and love, honor, and cherish them as the special gift that they are from God.

We've tried to share so many reassurances as well as warnings about the pitfalls of marriage. Please don't let it throw you. Being unaware is just as dangerous to your marriage as external threats or temptations. Use this information and learn from experience to not only avoid the mistakes, but to increase the intimacy of your relationship.

It's easy to allow yourself to get caught in the trap of culture's promiscuity, divorce, and remarriages. We call it the marriage-go-round. We know you've heard this before, but the only ones who win in divorce are the attorneys. But, Satan is the big winner. He hates marriages and will continue to do everything to destroy them.

If you'd take an honest assessment of the problems in your

marriage, you'd soon see that sin and rebellion have had an incredible influence. Otherwise, there'd be no cause for destructive conflict if God was placed as the head of your marriage and family. Yes, there will be disagreements, anger, and problems between you both, but that's natural and expected. We've mentioned Paul's words before about high emotions, and they're worth sharing again.

"Be angry, and do not sin":

do not let the sun go down on your wrath.

Ephesians 4:26

What usually gets in the way of a true happily ever after is the misconception that couples share about having problems. Most think that if they were "meant to be," then they'll never argue, slam a door, or refuse to talk it out during a fight. That's a fantasy. Couples with the greatest advantage for an everlasting relationship are those who have laid the foundations for communicating with each other no matter the situation or severity.

The best way to structure that foundation is to build your relationship upon The Five STONEs of Marriage. These simple rules of marriage are based on God's Word, and have been the golden seal, time-tested truths for a happily ever after relationship. Even if you've been blissfully married for years, these principles of Stance, Tension, Observation, Navigation and Effort promise to increase even the deepest of commitments.

Another resource that helps us daily are the marriage mentors we've grown close to. The reason clichés remain in our lexicon is because there is truth to them. Birds of a feather do flock together. In the most positive sense of this example are the opportunities to watch successful marriages happen in the lives of others who are willing to share their experiences.

Over the years we've connected with so many good folks who live the biblical marriage covenant. Does that mean they're perfect? No, not at all, but it does mean they're perfectly willing to open their hearts as trusted models of marriages that work.

Finally, please know that Leah and I are praying over you. It takes so much courage and sacrifice to recommit to marriage every day. It also takes a God-blessed spouse to hold the line for marriage and family. God knows the challenges you've both accepted to not only serve Him, but to serve each other. There is blessing in your marriage. Please allow God's anointing oil of eternal provision to pour over you and your marriage and know He has a wonderful plan for each of you and your marriage. It's God's own promise to you!

"For I know the plans I have for you," declares the Lord, "plans to prosper you and not to harm you, plans to give you hope and a future."

Jeremiah 29:11

ABOUT SCOTT & LEAH

Dr. Scott and Leah Silverii, have blended seven kids, a son-in-law and Lab/Golden named Winnie "You Better Not" Poo into a wonderfully unique family.

They are marriage champions and have dedicated their lives to growing, restoring and celebrating healthy, God centered covenant relationships.

They are both certified as Marriage On The Rock counselors and SYMBIS facilitators.

Scott, a retired chief of police, holds a PhD and post-doctoral hours from seminary. Leah is a New York Times and USA Today bestselling author of over 99 titles. Together they co-founded Five Stones Church in Midlothian, Texas where

Scott serves as senior pastor. They both teach marriage classes and are excited to share the Big Book of Marriage with you.

ALSO BY DR. SCOTT SILVERII

Favored Not Forgotten: Embrace the Season, Thrive in Obscurity, Activate Your Purpose

Unbreakable: From Past Pain To Future Glory

Retrain Your Brain - Using Biblical Meditation To Purify Toxic Thoughts

God Made Man - Discovering Your Purpose and Living an Intentional Life

Captive No More - Freedom From Your Past of Pain, Shame and Guilt

Broken and Blue: A Policeman's Guide To Health, Hope, and Healing

Life After Divorce: Finding Light In Life's Darkest Season

Police Organization and Culture: Navigating Law Enforcement in Today's Hostile Environment

The ABCs of Marriage: Devotional and Coloring Book

Love's Letters (A Collection of Timeless Relationship Advice from Today's Hottest Marriage Experts)

A First Responder Devotional

40 Days to a Better Firefighter Marriage

40 Days to a Better Military Marriage

40 Days to a Better Corrections Officer Marriage

40 Days to a Better 911 Dispatcher Marriage

40 Days to a Better EMT Marriage

40 Days to a Better Police Marriage

ACKNOWLEDGMENTS

We give all glory and praise to our heavenly Father. It was His son, Jesus Christ who lifted us up when we wanted to stay down, and the Holy Spirit who now pours life into our souls so that we may pour out into others.

God loves marriage, because He loves you!!!

www.ingramcontent.com/pod-product-compliance
Lightning Source LLC
Chambersburg PA
CBHW052130270326
41930CB00012B/2832